ON THIS DAY IN
ROCK 'N' ROLL

ON THIS DAY IN
ROCK 'N' ROLL

by
Sean Brickell
and
Rich Rothschild

**A Day-by-Day Calendar of the
Births, Deaths, and Major Events
of Rock History**

The Donning Company/Publishers
Norfolk/Virginia Beach

The Donning Company/Publishers
5659 Virginia Beach Boulevard
Norfolk, Virginia 23502

Library of Congress Cataloging in Publication Data

Brickell, Sean, 1951-
    The pages of rock and roll history.

        Includes index.
        1. Rock music — Chronology. I. Rothschild, Rich, 1956-   . II. title.
ML3534.B72   1983   784.5'4'009   83-1957
ISBN 0-89865-304-5

Previously printed under the title "The Pages of Rock History."
Revised May 1990

Dedication

With love for my wife, Robin "Bean" Brickell; our children Alex and Lesley; my mother Betty and father Edward Brickell; Heidi, Michael, Rachel and the soon-to-be-born Ullrich; Jean and Ed Snyder, David and Margaret Kimmel, Keith "Hoss" and Judi Hathaway; and Samantha Stokes.

For friendship: Jerry Davis; Larry Phillips; Larry and Martha Mednick; Linda Branche; Jeff Halik; Kim Cosner; Dawn Foster; Belinda Tompkins; Tracey Alexander; Kathie Moore; Claire Kaufman; Bill Mertz; Ron Gregory; Ann Stefanik; Marc Mirman; Joe Pulley; Chris Lane; Barry Friedman; Mike Cook, and Bill Reid.

For musical inspiration: Van Morrison; John Lennon; Miles Davis; Bruce Springsteen; Bruce Hornsby; Sam Cooke; Elvis; Tom Waits; Ella Fitzgerald; Bryan Ferry; Louis Armstrong; and Dave Edmunds.

And, of course, my partner Rich and his wife Lynda Rothschild, and Stanley Hainer, our publisher.

— Sean Brickell

To Lynda, my wife; our families, especially my parents Walter and Vivian, for their support in my early rock 'n' roll habits and so much more; Bruce Springsteen and my little rocker Lindsay Rose Rothschild, my daughter.

— Rich Rothschild

Acknowledgments

Special thanks to David Kimmel, Carly Stanley, Circe Rhi, Cliff Korradi, Miles Davis, John Lennon, Ralph King, Paul Fussell, IBM Correcting Selectric III, Eric Feber, Hoss and Judi, Chris Lane, Rick Miller, Ron Swan, Van Wycoff, Big Steve C, Chuck Applebach, Larry and Martha, David Hollingsworth, Randy Allen, Heidi Ellen Robinson, Bill Mertz (for the cover photos), Roy Rosenberg, Dr. Conrad Festa, Steve Fischer, Ron Herbert, Joe Pulley, the music community of Virginia, and the many publicity folks at the record labels who provided bios and photos through the years.

Also to Bob Friedman and Doug Kahle for the much-needed guidance and answers to our questions.

Recognition to the memory of Jim Morrison for showing me how to "Break On Through (To The Other Side)" and understand limits.

— Sean Brickell

Special thanks for friendship, help, and support to Jim Chiado, Ed Cockrell, Lee Demsey, Debbie Fricka, Lisa Julig, Terry Bass, Moshe Mendelowitz, and Ken Rothschild (for legal services and turning me on to FM radio when I was eleven).

For their inspiration: air staff of WNEW FM (mid-seventies), Camp Shawnee, The Rascals, The Doors, Creedence Clearwater Revival, and (most of all) Bruce Springsteen and The E Street Band.

Also to Bob Friedman and Doug Kahle.

— Rich Rothschild

Introduction

There is magic that is rock 'n' roll! The excitement, the sounds, the feeling of rock extend beyond the music, the stars, or the events; they become a spirit. With this spirit we bring you *On This Day in Rock 'n' Roll*.

From Allan Freed, the Cleveland disc jockey of the fifties who coined the phrase "Rock 'n' Roll," to the bands of today, there has been a common spirit.

It's this spirit when Bruce Springsteen jumps into the audience to sing "Tenth Avenue Freeze Out"; when the Mets win the World Series; when Paul McCartney and Stevie Wonder make records together.

On This Day in Rock 'n' Roll is a day-by-day account of the evolution of the rock spirit. Entries include births, deaths, major recording release dates, initial record chart debuts, and events relative to the history and spirit of rock. Each day demonstrates the power, the energy, the drive that's rock 'n' roll.

Many entires are of people who never created a note of music or had a behind-the-scenes role. Many events couldn't be further from a concert or recording session. The key to their listings is the spirit they had.

Stonewall Jackson was a rocker, though he never played rock and died almost a century before its birth. He had the spirit of rock: a direct, fast, determined lifestyle with a driven cause. He died young pursuing his dream, advancing toward it full boogie. His character is the same as that found in Jim Morrison, Janis Joplin, Pete Townshend, and John Lennon. They shared an inner quality.

Even within these broad rock definitions, not everyone fits. Many successful people and things aren't rockers. We do not attempt to assign a value to our entries or those omitted. We just want to categorize rock-class items. *The London Times* newspaper is a rocker, but not *The Christian Science Monitor*. Pablo Picasso was a rocker, but not James Audubon. "Happy Days" is a rock TV show; not so "The Waltons." *Star Wars* is a rock flick, but not *Xanadu*.

If a ballad by The Beatles has touched your heart, if you've followed Bruce Springsteen's concert tour from city to city, if you ever camped overnight to see The Rolling Stones, if you're the first in the record store to buy Bob Seger's new release, then you live the spirit of rock. You understand *On This Day in Rock 'n' Roll*, and we know you!

We've been gathering information for our book most of our lives, although we didn't begin with plans for a book. We have an insatiable love of rock music, live and recorded, and we love rock trivia. About three years ago Rich started writing down our rock entries. A few entries may be obscure enough to get you to phone your favorite radio station and test its rock history knowledge.

Record release dates generally came from artists' record labels. "Charting" means the first appearance on a *Billboard Magazine* single or album chart, using the issue's weekly date.

Rock is alive and growing and brings us new entries almost daily. We gather information everywhere, as we always have. At times we find an important entry we had never listed. History is never-ending. Please contact us if we've missed something. Maybe we overemphasize rock's value, but millions share our enthusiasm. We see people like us in every city, every country.

We accept ultimate responsibility for the entries. We did not intentionally leave out any major person or event, and many entries are admittedly subjective.

History doesn't make an evenly-distributed package; more happens some days than others. Please don't think we "prepared" poorly for your birthday, as some people actually have claimed. We didn't create data, we only record and report it.

More than anything, we hope you'll have as much fun with *On This Day in Rock 'n' Roll* as we've had gathering the information. We managed to inject a little subtle humor in some of our entries. You're on our wavelength if they make you smile instead of sending you into a rage. That's our sense of humor working on you, and thanks for noticing.

— Sean Brickell
— Rich Rothschild

JANUARY

January 1

New Year's Day

Born: Country Joe McDonald (1942)   *The London Times* (1788)
Paul Revere (1735)   J. Edgar Hoover (1895)
Betsy Ross (1752)

Died: Hank Williams, heart failure (1953)

Events: *The Beatles* have their first record company audition. A record executive told their manager, "These boys won't make it. Guitar groups are out. Go back to Liverpool, Mr. Epstein. You have a good business there" (1962).

Simon and Garfunkel's "Sound of Silence" reaches No. 1 (1966).

"Doonesbury" comic strip, with 65 million readers, goes on vacation, as creator Gary Trudeau gives the characters 20 months to "grow up" (1983).

January 2

Born: Roger Miller (1936)   Chick Churchill, *Ten Years After* (1942)

Events: *Yankee Doodle Dandy* opens starring Jimmy Cagney, who goes on to become the first actor to win an Oscar for a musical (1942).

Mobile Fidelity releases "Abbey Road" at half speed (1981).

Annie closes on Broadway after 2,377 performances (1983).

January 3

Born: George Martin, *The Beatles'* producer (1926)
Van Dyke Parks (1941)

Stephen Stills (1945)
John Paul Jones, *Led Zeppelin* (1945)

Died: Edgar Cayce (1945)
Jack Ruby (1967)

Mal Evans, *Beatles* roadie (1976)

Events: United States breaks diplomatic relations with Cuba (1961).

First Acid Test takes place at Fillmore Auditorium in San Francisco (1966).

New Jersey declares John Lennon and Yoko Ono's "Two Virgins" LP cover obscene (both are naked); 30,000 copies are confiscated (1969).

Jimi Hendrix plays on "Lulu Show," BBC (1969).

Bob Dylan kicks off major tour in Chicago (1974).

Elvis Costello releases "Armed Forces," the first gold New Wave LP (1979).

Warner/Elektra/Atlantic Records lowers 1,000 catalogue LPs from $8.98 to $6.98 (1983).

January 4

Born: Volker Hornback, *Tangerine Dream* (1944)

Events: First Top 100 Chart published by *Billboard Magazine*, (1936).

Elvis Presley cuts two demos for his mother, his first ever, at Sun Studios, Memphis: "Casual Love" and "I'll Never Stand In Your Way" (1954).

Russia buys wheat from the United States for the first time (1964).

"Performance," Mick Jagger's first film effort, is released in England, two years after its completion (1971).

January 5

Born: Sam Phillips, Sun Records owner (1923)
Walter Mondale (1928)

FM frequency radio is first demonstrated (1940)
Chris Stein, *Blondie* (1950)

Died: Charles Mingus of Gehrig's Disease (1979)

January 6

Born: Joan of Arc (1412)
Sherlock Holmes (1845)
Danny Thomas (1914)
Wilbert Harrison (1929)

Syd Barrett, founder and
"Crazy Diamond" of
Pink Floyd (1946)

Events: Morse demonstrates the telegraph for the first time (1838).

The Rolling Stones begin their first tour headlining with *The Ronettes* opening (1964).

"Happening '68," a variety show of assorted rock stars, appears on TV (1968).

January 7

Born: Kenny Loggins (1948)

Events: First nationwide United States election (1789).

First intercontinental phone call: New York to London (1927).

After seven months of filming, the multi-million dollar production of *Ben Hur* is completed (1959).

"Snoopy vs. The Red Baron" LP is released by *The Royal Guardsmen* (1967).

"The Beat Goes On" by Sonny and Cher is released (1967).

Ron Wood hosts an educational and musical event at Town Hall in New York City. Billed as "An Evening With Rolling Stone Ron Wood," tickets go for $17.50 to $30 and include a party at the Magique Disco afterward (1983).

January 8

Born: Elvis Presley (1935)
Shirley Bassey (1937)
"Little Anthony" Gourdine,
*Little Anthony and the
Imperials* (1941)
Lee Jackson, *The Nice* (1943)

Robbie Krieger, *The Doors*
(1946)
Terry Sylvester, *The Hollies*
(1947)
David Bowie (1947)

Events: CBS Records and Sony demonstrate "Video 45," a four-song video cassette, at the annual Consumer Electronics Show. Japan has already sold more than 32,000 for a price of $15 to $19 (1983).

January 9

Born: Richard Nixon (1913)   Jimmy Page, *Led Zeppelin* (1944)
Joan Baez (1941)   David Johanson (1950)

Events: *Little Caesar* opens, starring Edward G. Robinson. Clark Gable read for the part, but Darryl F. Zanuck said, "His ears are too big. He looks like an ape!" (1931).

Lou Reed marries a waitress named Betty (1973).

UNICEF Concert is held to help needy children (1979).

January 10

Born: Ray Bolger (1904)   Rod Stewart (1945)
Jerry Wexler, producer (1917)   Donny Hathaway (1945)
Max Roach (1925)   Donald Fagen (1948)
Johnny Ray (1927)   George Foreman (1949)
Ronnie Hawkins (1935)   Pat Benatar (1952)
Sal Mineo (1939)
Jim Croce (1942)

Died: Howlin' Wolf, in Chicago (1976)

Events: United Nations General Assembly first meets in London (1946).

Atlantic Records, a rhythm and blues label, is formed by Herb Abramson, president, and Ahmet Ertegun, vice president (1948).

Bob Dylan appears on television with Earl Scruggs (1971).

Elektra/Asylum Records is dissolved as Atlantic and Warner Brothers Records absorb the roster (1983).

Tennessee's governor decrees "Elvis Presley Day" (1983).

"Maneater" is the fifth No. 1 song by *Hall and Oates,* the most ever for a duo (1983).

January 11

Born: Bobby Goldsboro (1941)   Maggie Bell 91945)
            Slim Harpo (1942)
            Clarence Clemons, *E Street*
            Band (1942)

Events: *Ziegfeld Follies,* Fred Astaire's nineteenth film, opens. It is his first in
            color, as well as the first time he and Gene Kelly work together (1946).

            The first disco, Whiskey-A-Go-Go, opens in Los Angeles (1963).

            The Surgeon General announces that cigarette smoking is hazardous
            to your health (1954).

            "Dark Side of the Moon" by *Pink Floyd* hits the 400th week on *Billboard*'s
            Top 200 charts, an unequalled feat (1982).

January 12

Born: Long John Baldry [6 feet,   "Smokin' Joe" Frazier (1944)
            7 inches] (1941)   George Duke (1946)

Events: Rin Tin Tin successfully makes the transition from the silent screen to
            "talkies" with *Million Dollar Collar* release (1929).

            "Please Please Me" is released by *The Beatles* in the United Kingdom.
            A month later it reaches No. 1, their first (1963).

            "Hullabuloo" premieres on ABC-TV (1965).

            Frank Zappa spends $300,000 of his personal money to record with the
            London Symphony Orchestra for his Barking Pumpkin label (1983).

January 13

Born: Robert Stack (1919)   Suggs, *Madness* (1961)

Died: Stephen Foster, after tripping over a washbasin on New York's
            Bowery. He had been drinking, and nobody recognized him when he
            got to the hospital (1864).

            Wyatt Earp, in Los Angeles (1929)

            Donny Hathaway (1979)

Events: "Duke of Earl" by Gene Chandler charts (1962).

            Adam West and Burt Ward star as the Caped Crusader and the Boy
            Wonder in the television debut of "Batman" (1966).

            "Sunshine of Your Love" by *Cream* charts — their first hit (1968).

            Eric Clapton's Rainbow Concert in London (1973).

January 14

Born: Benedict Arnold (1741)   Faye Dunaway (1941)
           Albert Schweitzer (1875)   Tim Harris, *The Foundations*
           Jack Jones (1938)   (1948)
           Allen Toussaint (1938)

Died: Jeanette McDonald (1965)

Events: Hayes (film censorship) office opens (1922).

"The Twist" by Chubby Checker charts for the second time (1962).

The Beatles release "I Want To Hold Your Hand" (1964).

Bill Graham leases the Fillmore Auditorium in San Francisco. The first show is a benefit for area mime troupes (1966).

The first "Be-In" is held at Golden Gate Park in San Francisco (1967).

The Doors' premiere LP is released with "Break On Through" as the first single (1967).

"So You Want To Be A Rock 'N' Roll Star" by *The Byrds* is released (1967).

Paul Gadd (was known as Paul Raven, now Gary Glitter) lowers all the Paul Raven recordings locked in a coffin into the Thames, official ending the life of Paul Raven (1973).

The last *Sex Pistols* concert is held at Winterland, San Francisco (1978).

The final episode of M*A*S*H is filmed, Stage 9, 20th Century Fox Studios (1983).

January 15

Born: Gene Krupa (1909)   Don Van Vliet [Captain
           Lloyd Bridges (1913)   Beefheart] (1941)
           Chuck Berry (1926)   Ronnie Van Zant, *Lynyrd*
           Martin Luther King (1929)   *Skynyrd* (1948)

Died: Meyer Lansky (1983)

Events: *The Who's* first single "I Can't Explain/Bad Headed Woman" is released by Decca. Only 1,000 are pressed, but within six weeks more than 100,000 are sold.

The Rolling Stones on "The Ed Sullivan Show" sing "Let's Spend Some Time Together." The song is "Let's Spend The Night..."

"Happy Days" premieres on TV (1974).

Graham Parker concert is broadcast on MTV from Chicago (1983).

January 16

Born: Ethel Merman (1909)   Bob Vogle, *The Ventures* (1937)
             Marilyn Horne (1934)   Sandy Denny (1947)

Events: The Cavern Club opens in Liverpool, England. *The Beatles* would get there start there (1958).

Hello Dolly opens on Broadway (1964).

Paul McCartney is busted for possessing six ounces of pot in Tokyo; he spends ten days in jail (1980).

Jefferson Starship raises $10,000 for Walden House Drug Rehabilitation Center in San Francisco by auctioning rock memorabilia (1983).

January 17

Born: Ben Franklin (1706)   William Hart, *The Delfonics*
             Al Capone (1899)   (1945)
             Muhammad Ali (1942)   Mick Taylor, ex-*Rolling Stones*
                                           (1948)

Died: Billy Stewart (1970)

Events: Jackie Coogan's first flick, *The Kid,* opens and he becomes a star (1921).

The first jazz concert is held at New York's Metropolitan Opera House (1944).

Four American B-52s carrying four A-bombs crash off Spain's coast (1966).

January 18

Born: A. A. Milne, author of *Winnie*   Elmore James (1918)
             the Pooh (1904)   David Ruffin, *The Temptations*
             Cary Grant [Archibald   (1941)
             Alexander Leach] (1904)   Bobby Goldsboro (1941)

Events: *The Rolling Stones* perform a benefit concert for Nicaraguan earthquake victims (1973).

Wendy O. Williams, *The Plasmatics,* is arrested in Milwaukee for simulating masturbation with a sledgehammer before an audience. The police beat her up (1981).

Jim Thorpe posthumously receives his Olympic medals (1983).

January 19

Born: Robert E. Lee (1807)   Janis Joplin (1943)
             Edgar Allen Poe (1809)   Dolly Parton (1946)
             Phil Everly (1939)   Robert Palmer (1949)

Events: *Dire Straits'* first LP is released and later goes platinum (1979).

January 20

Born: George Burns (1895)   Paul Stanley, *Kiss* (1952)
             George Grantham, *Poco* (1947)

Died: Allan Freed, Rock 'n' Roll's first   Jackie Wilson (1984)
             DJ. He coined the phras
             "Rock 'n' Roll" (1965).

Events: The Revolutionary War ends (1783).

             Warner Baxter wins the first Academy Award for best actor in *Old Arizona* (1929).

             John F. Kennedy is inaugurated President and tells America to "Ask not what your country can do for you....Rather what you can do for your country." (1961).

             The Beatles' first United States album, "Meet The Beatles," is released (1964).

             The fifty-two American hostages are released after 444 days in Iran (1981).

             Ozzy Osbourne bites the head off a dead bat that a fan had tossed on stage in Des Moines. He cancels his tour and has rabies treatments (1982).

January 21

Born: T. J. "Stonewall" Jackson (1824)   Edwin Starr (1942)
             Huddie "Leadbelly" Ledbetter   Jimmy Ibbotson, *The Dirt Band*
               (1885)   (1947)
             Richie Havens (1941)

Died: George Orwell (1950)

Events: George Harrison and Patricia Anne Boyd marry (1966).

January 22

Born: Lord George Gordon Byron (1788)
D. W. Griffith (1875)
Steve Adler, ex-Guns N' Roses (1965)

Sam Cooke (1931)
Oliver (1945)
Steve Perry, *Journey* (1953)

Events: Buddy Holly does his last recording ever: within two weeks he dies in a plane crash. Holly's last songs are recorded solo in his home and include "Peggy Sue Got Married" (1959).

January 23

Born: Ernie Kovaks (1919)
Jerry Lawson, *The Persuasions* (1944)
Richard Dean Anderson, Mac Gyver (1950)

Danni Federici, *E Street Band* (1950)
Robin Zander, *Cheap Trick* (1953)

Died: Terry Kath, accidentally shot himself in Chicago (1978).

Events: *The Treasure of the Sierra Madre* opens (1948).

Bjorn Borg announces his retirement from tennis competiton at age twenty-six (1983).

Charlie Daniels hosts the ninth Volunteer Jam in Tennessee (1983).

January 24

Born: Doug Kershaw (1936)
Ray Stevens (1941)
Neil Diamond (1944)

Warren Zevon (1947)
John Belushi (1949)

Died: James "Shep" Shepherd, *Shep and The Limelites,* found in his car beaten (1970).

Events: Gold first found in California (1848).

The Beatles sign their management contract with Brian Epstein (1962).

The last Buddy Holly tour starts.

January 25

Born: Gary Brian Tibbs, *Adam and The Ants* (1958)

God (later renamed China), daughter of Grace Slick and Paul Kantner of *The Jefferson Airplane,* later renamed *Jefferson Starship* (1971)

Events: The first Emmy Awards show (1949).

"Proud Mary" by *Creedence Clearwater Revival* charts (1969).

January 26

Born: General Douglas MacArthur (1880)
Paul Newman (1925)

Jules Feiffer (1929)
Huey "Piano" Smith (1934)
Corky Laing, *Mountain* (1948)

Died: Paul "Bear" Bryant (1983)

Events: Buddy Holly makes his first recordings (1956).

Buddy Holly and the Crickets appear on "The Ed Sullivan Show" (1958).

Frank Sinatra plays before the largest audience ever gathered for a single performer, 175,000, in Rio de Janeiro (1980).

January 27

Born: Wolfgang A. Mozart (1756)
Donna Reed (1921)
Bobby Bland (1930)
Nick Mason, *Pink Floyd* (1945)

Nadra Talley, *The Ronettes* (1947)
Chuck Larsen, *Snuff* (1948)

Died: Mahalia Jackson

Michael Patrick Hilon, 2'10", forty-five-pound midget who played E.T., of pneumonia (1983).

Events: Public television broadcasts for the first time (1926).

Vietnam cease-fire is signed in Paris (1973).

Capricorn Records files for bankruptcy (1980).

Records with allegedly hidden messages when played backward would carry warning labels under a bill introduced in the Arkansas House (1983).

George Harrison in the *London Sun* says, "We were a bunch of loonies, taking drugs and trying to be honest" (1983).

January 28

Born: Arthur Rubinstein (1886)

Died: Freddie Prinze [accidentally shot himself] (1977)

Events: Gary Glitter [Paul Gadd] retires (1976).

"Between The Buttons" by *The Rolling Stones* is released (1967).

"For What It's Worth" by *Buffalo Springfield* charts (1967).

January 29

Born: Anton Chekhov (1860)   David Byron, *Uriah Heep* (1947)
Paddy Chayefsky (1923)   Tom Selleck (1945)

Events: Stevie Nicks weds Kim Anderson (1983).

Chrissie Hynde and Ray Davies have their first baby (1983).

January 30

Born: Franklin Delano Roosevelt   Marty Balin [Martin Jere
(1880)   Buchwald], *Jefferson Starship*
Ruth Brown (1928)   (1945)
Joe Terranoua, *Danny and the*   Steve Marriott (1947)
Juniors (1941)

Died: Jesse Fuller [San Francisco blues great] (1976)
Professor Longhair [King of New Orleans music] (1980)
Lightning Hopkins [of cancer] (1982)

Events: *The Beatles* film and record "Let It Be" atop Apple Records' Abbey
Roads studio (1969).

MCA buys ABC Records (1979).

January 31

Born: Jackie Robinson (1919)   Johnny Rotten, *Sex Pistols* (1956)
Norman Mailer (1923)   Phil Collins, *Genesis* (1951)
Terry Kath, *Chicago* (1948)
Phil Manzanera, *Roxy Music*
(1951)

Died: Slim Harpo (1970)

Events: Cuba is voted out of Organization of American States (1962).

Paul McCartney signs with CBS Records for a reported $20 million
(1979).

Eric Carr,
Gene Simmons,
Paul Stanley and
Bruce Kulick

FEBRUARY

February 1

Born: Clark Gable (1901)
Bob Shane, *Kingston Trio* (1934)
Ray "Dr. Hook" Sawyer (1937)
Don Everly (1937)
Jimmy Carl Black,
   Mothers of Invention (1938)

Tommy Duffy, *Echos* (1944)
Lisa Marie Presley [Elvis' sole
   heir] (1968)

Events: Daniel Defoe's Robinson Crusoe is rescued (1709).

"Why Do Fools Fall In Love," Frankie Lymon's first hit, charts (1956).

Black students in North Carolina stage the first lunch counter sit-in at Woolworth's (1960).

The Misfits, Clark Gable and Marilyn Monroe's last film, opens (1961).

"I Want To Hold Your Hand" hits No. 1 for *The Beatles* in the United States (1961).

P. J. Proby is banned by ABC, the large British theater chain, after several episodes of his trousers splitting on stage (1965).

Buick begins to offer eight-track stereo in their cars as dealer options (1967).

February 2

Born: Lonnie Johnson (1869)
Stan Getz (1927)
Skip Batten, *The Byrds* (1934)
Graham Nash (1942)

Peter MacBeth, *The
   Foundations* (1943)
Alphonso Johnson [jazz
   bassist] (1951)

Died: Sid Vicious, *The Sex Pistols,* of a drug overdose (1979).

Sam Chatman [elder statesman of the blues] (1983).

Events: The first motion picture close-up film, *Fred Ott's Sneeze.* Fred Ott was a studio assistant at Thomas Edison's studio, and the film featured Fred's nose and handkerchief (1893).

RCA issues the first 45 RPM record, beginning the decline of 78 RPM (1949).

The Beatles' first tour date is held in Gaumont, Bradford. The headliner was Helen Shapiro (1963).

The "Midnight Special" premieres on NBC-TV (1973).

REO Speedwagon's "High Fidelity" goes platinum (1981).

February 3

Born: Gertrude Stein (1874)   Dave Davies, *Kinks* (1947)
            Johnny "Guitar" Watson (1935)   Melanie (1947)
            Shawn Phillips [Jesus Christ
                Superstar] (1943)

Died: Buddy Holly, J. P. "Big Bopper" Richardson, and Richie Valens in a
            plane crash outside of Mason City, Iowa. They were en route to a
            concert in Fargo, North Dakota when the plane went down in a
            cornfield in Ames, Iowa (1959).

            Alex Harvey (1982)

Events: The "Star Spangled Banner" is declared the national anthem (1931).

            Disney's *The Three Caballeros,* the first full-length, feature film to
            combine animation and live action, opens (1945).

            All of *The Beatles,* except Paul McCartney, hire Allen Klein as their
            manager (1969).

February 4

Born: Charles Lindbergh (1902)   Alice Cooper (1948)
            John Steel, *The Animals* (1941)   Jerry Shirley, *Humble Pie* (1952)
            Johnny Gamble, *The Classics*   Steve Hackett (1950)
                (1942)

Died: Karen Carpenter [heart failure] (1983)

Events: The first talking film, *The Jazz Singer* starring Al Jolson, is released
            (1927).

            The Beatles appoint Eastman and Eastman as Apple's general council.
            One partner is Linda (then Eastman) McCartney's father (1969).

February 5

Born: Red Buttons (1919)   Sven Johnson, ex-*Tangerine
            Ron Wilson, *Joy of Cooking*   Dream* (1943)
                (1933)   Al Kooper (1944)
            Hank Aaron [most hits record: Bob Marley (1945)
                total bases] (1934)   Nigel Olsson, ex-*Elton John
            Alex Harvey (1935)   Band* (1949)
            Duff Mc Kagan, Guns 'N' Roses (1964)
Events: *Woman of the Year,* the first Spencer Tracy/Katharine Hepburn flick,
            opens (1942).

            Gene Pitney's first hit, "Love My Life Away," charts (1961).

            Peter Frampton weds Barbara Goldberg (1983).

February 6

Born: Babe Ruth (1894)   Fabian (1943)
W. Axl Rose, Guns N'Roses (1962)

Events: "Ferry Cross The Mersey" by *Gerry and the Pacemakers* charts (1965).

February 7

Born: Charles Dickens (1812)   Lawrence Ascott, *Isotope* (1946)
Eubie Blake (1883)   Jimmy Greenspan (1948)

Events: *The Beatles* make their first visit to the United States (1964).

George Harrison has his tonsils removed (1965).

February 8

Born: Jules Verne (1828)   Jim Capaldi, *Traffic* (1944)
James Dean (1931)   Adolpho "Fito" de la Parra,
John Williams [*Star Wars, E.T.,*   *Canned Heat* (1946)
and *Superman* soundtrack   Ted Turner, *Wishbone Ash*
composer] (1932)   (1950)
Tom Rush (1941)   Cindy Wilson, *B-52s* (1957)
Vince Neil, ex - Motley Crue

Events: "I Saw Her Standing There" charts for *The Beatles* (1964).

February 9

Born: Carole King (1941)   Mia Farrow (1945)

Died: Gabby Hayes (1969)   Bill Haley [first rock superstar]
(1981)

Events: *The Beatles* make their first "Ed Sullivan Show" appearance for $2,400 (1964).

"The Heroes of Rock 'N' Roll is broadcast on ABC-TV (1979).

February 10

Born: Roberta Flack (1940)   Don Wilson, *The Ventures* (1937)
Cliff Burton, Metallica (1962)

Events: *Sly and the Family Stone*'s first hit, "Dance To The Music," charts (1968).

Producer Phil Spector nearly dies in an auto accident in Los Angeles (1970).

February 11

Born: Thomas Edison (1847)   Burt Reynolds (1936)
Josh White (1908)   Gerry Goffin (1939)
Gene Vincent (1935)   Sergio Mendez (1941)

Events: *The Beatles'* first recording session with George Martin lasts twelve hours and produces "Please, Please Me" (1962).

The Beatles' first United States concert in the Washington, D.C., Coliseum. The songs: "Twist and Shout," "All My Lovin'," "From Me To You," "Roll Over Beethoven," "I Saw Her Standing There," "This Boy," "I Want To Hold Your Hand," "Till There Was You," "Please, Please Me," "I Want To Be Your Man," "Long Tall Sally," and "She Loves You" (1964).

Ringo Starr marries Maureen Cox (1965).

"Elvis" (ABC-TV), competing against *Gone With The Wind* and *One Flew Over the Cuckoo's Nest,* creates the most expensive night in network programming history (1979).

The Rolling Stones' "Let's Spend The Night Together" movie opens (1983).

February 12

Born: Charles Darwin (1809)   Stanley Knight, *Black Oak*
Abe Lincoln (1809)   *Arkansas* (1949)
Lorne Greene (1915)   Steve Hackett, ex-*Genesis*
Ray Manzarek, *The Doors*   (1950)
(1935)

Died: Sal Mineo [murdered] (1976)   Alberto Vargas (1983)
Eubie Blake (1983)

Events: *The Beatles* play Carnegie Hall (1964).

February 13

Born: Tennessee Ernie Ford (1919)   Ed Gagliardi, ex-*Foreigner*
Peter Tork, *The Monkees* (1946)   (1952)

Events: *The Rolling Stones* appear on "The Ed Sullivan Show" (1966).

Bob Dylan plays the Los Angeles Forum and records much of "Wake of the Flood" (1972).

Cabaret opens on film (1972).

February 14

Born:
Jack Benny (1894)
Hugh Downs (1921)
Magic Sam [Chicago bluesman] (1937)

Vic Briggs, *The Animals* (1945)
Tim Buckley (1947)
Alan Hunter, MTV Video Jock

Died:
Several gangsters in the infamous St. Valentine's Day Massacre (1929).

Mike Bloomfield of a drug overdose (1981).

Events:
Jackie Kennedy gives a TV tour of the White House (1964).

"Twist and Shout" charts for *The Beatles* (1964).

Albert Grossman, Janis Joplin's manager, goes to court to prove her death was an accident, not suicide. He had a $250,000 insurance policy on her (1971).

A judge rules that *The Life and Times of Xaviera Hollander* cannot use "The Mickey Mouse Club Theme" as the musical background for an orgy scene (1975).

Lawyers for eight record companies file fifty-two suits accusing 130 people of pirate recordings in North Carolina, the largest roundup ever (1983).

February 15

Born:
John Barrymore (1882)
Brian Holland (1941)
Jane Seymour (1951)

Mick Avory, *Kinks* (1944)
Melissa Manchester (1951)

Died:
Nat King Cole (1965)

Little Walter (1968)

Events:
"Glad All Over" charts for *The Dave Clark Five* (1964).

Paul McCartney loses four-year battle on publishing for "Yesterday," "Hey Jude," "Eleanor Rigby," and "Let It Be." He sold them for $25 million in 1969 and was rejected in his $30 million offer to repurchase them (1983).

Freddie Fender files for bankruptcy (1983).

February 16

Born:
Edgar Bergman (1903)
Sonny Bono (1935)
Le Var Burton (1957)

Andy Taylor, *Duran Duran* (1961)

Events:
The first radio newscast (1923).

Paul Anka marries Ann Dezogheb (1963).

February 17

Born: Gene Pitney (1941)

Died: Geronimo (1909)   Thelonious Monk [jazz great] of a heart attack] (1982)

Events: "Surfin'" hits the charts for *The Beach Boys* (1962).

Joni Mitchell announces her retirement after a concert in London's Royal Albert Hall. It wasn't (1970).

February 18

Born: Yoko Ono (1933)   John Travolta (1954)
Rob Bachman, *Bachman-Turner Overdrive* (1953)

Events: The first opera opens in the United States (1735).

The Olympics in Squaw Valley is the first to be covered live on TV (1960).

"Psycho Killer" charts by *The Talking Heads* (1978).

February 19

Born: Lee Marvin (1924)   Mama Cass Elliott (1943)
William "Smokey" Robinson (1940)   Tony Iommi, *Black Sabbath* (1948)
Lou Christie (1943)   Mark Andes, *Firefall* (1948)

Died: Bon Scott, *AC/DC*, of an alcohol overdose (1981).

Events: The phonograph is patented (1878).

Kris Kristofferson weds Lisa Meyers (1983).

February 20

Born: Buffy Saint-Marie (1941)   Walter Becker, *Steely Dan* (1950)
Jerome "J" Geils (1946)   Patty Hearst (1954)

Events: John Glenn becomes the first American to orbit the earth (1962).

"Go Now" is the first chart-maker for *The Moody Blues* (1965).

Ringo stars in his first non-Beatle movie, *Candy* (1968).

Pat Benatar and Neil Geraldo wed (1982).

February 21

Born: Nina Simone (1933)
David Geffen (1943)
Ron Nagle (1939)

Jerry Harrison, *Talking Heads* (1949)

Died: Malcolm X (Little) is assassinated in the Audubon Ballroom, New York City (1965).

Murray "The K" Kauffman, the fifth Beatle, of cancer (1982).

Events: Nixon arrives in China (1972); and again (1976).

February 22

Born: George Washington (1732)
Robert Young (1907)

Edward Kennedy (1932)

Events: The first record of English colonists eating popcorn (1630).

Carl Perkins' first hit, "Blue Suede Shoes," makes the charts (1956).

Elvis' first hit, "Heartbreak Hotel," charts (1956).

February 23

Born: George Frederick Handel (1685)
Peter Fonda (1939)

Johnny Winter (1944)
Brad Whitford, *Aerosmith* (1952)

Events: The Russian Revolution begins in St. Petersburg [Leningrad] (1917).

Herschel Walker, Heisman Trophy winner, signs with the USFL's New Jersey Generals in football's most lucrative offer, $8 million plus (1983).

February 24

Born: Sidney Poitier (1924)
Michel Legrand (1932)
Nicky Hopkins [keyboard session genius] (1944)

Paul Jones, *Manfred Mann* (1944)

Events: The first Sherlock Holmes movie, a one-reeler with Clive Brook as Holmes, is released (1929).

February 25

Born Enrico Caruso (1873)   Stuart Wood, *Bay City Rollers*
         George Harrison (1943)   (1957)
         Elkie Brooks (1945)

Events: "That'll Be The Day" is recorded by Buddy Holly (1957).

Cassius Clay defeats Sonny Liston in seven rounds and becomes "The Greatest" (1964).

"Penny Lane/Strawberry Fields" is released by *The Beatles* (1967).

"Plastic Letters" by Blondie is released (1978).

February 26

Born: Buffalo Bill Cody (1846)   Godfrey Cambridge (1933)
         Jackie "The Great One"   Paul Cotton, *Poco* (1943)
           Gleason (1916)   Bob "Bear" Hite, *Canned Heat*
         Fats Domino (1928)   (1945)
         Johnny Cash (1932)

February 27

Born: John Steinbeck (1902)   Joanne Woodward (1932)
         Elizabeth Taylor (1932)   Ralph Nader (1934)
         Neal Schon (1959)

Events: "I'm Walkin'" by Fats Domino charts (1957).

Keith Richard is busted for heroin in Toronto (1977).

February 28

Born: Zero Mostel (1926)   Brian Jones (1942)
         John Fahey (1939)   Joe South (1942)

Events: *Palooka* opens and introduces Jimmy Durante and "Inka Dinka Do" (1934).

The Cavern Club in Liverpool, where *The Beatles* got their start, closes with $10,000 in debts. The stage is cut in pieces and sold to fans (1966).

M*A*S*H broadcasts final episode to largest TV audience in history. After eleven years of successful ratings, advertisers break all-time high scale by paying up to $450,000 for thirty seconds of commercial time (1983).

February 29

Born: Jimmy Dorsey (1904)

Events: John Lennon's visa to the United States expires, and he begins his battle to obtain residency (1972).

Alex
Lifeson

Neil
Peart

Geddy
Lee

MARCH

March 1

Born: Chopin (1809)   Ralph Towner (1940)
              Dinah Shore (1917)   Roger Daltrey (1944)
              Harry Belafonte (1927)

Events: The first Sun record, an alto sax duet, is released and goes nowhere (1952).

              John Kennedy creates the Peace Corps (1961).

              Mattel Toys places Ken dolls on sale as Barbie's boyfriend (1961).

              Jim Morrison allegedly "exposes organs" in southern Florida concert (1969).

              Patti Smith and "Sonic" Smith wed (1980).

March 2

Born: Sam Houston (1793)   George Benson (1943)
              Kurt Weill (1900)   Lou Reed (1944)
              Dr. Seuss (1904)   Rory Gallagher (1949)
              Desi Arnaz (1917)
              Willie Chambers, *Chambers
              Brothers,* (1938)

Died: Charlie Christian (1942)

Events: The movie *The Sound of Music* opens (1965).

              "Wooly Bully" becomes *Sam the Sham and the Pharaohs'* first chart-maker (1965).

              Jim Morrison is arrested after his concert of March 1, and charged with "lewd behavior" on six counts, including public exposure, public masturbation, and ejaculation (1969).

              Havana Jam, sponsored by CBS Records, features Billy Joel, Stephen Stills, Weather Report, and others (1979).

March 3

Born: Alexander Graham Bell (1847)   Janice Garfat, *Dr. Hook* (1944)
Vincent Van Gogh (1853)   Angus Wilson, *AC/DC*
Herman "Jr." Parker (1927)

Events: "Bits and Pieces" by *The Dave Clark Five* charts (1964).

Buffalo Springfield officially forms (1966).

"Something Stupid" by Frank and Nancy Sinatra charts (1967).

A member of Hell's Angels testifies that the club has tried "at least three times to kill Mick Jagger because of the Altamont 1969 concert problems" (1983).

March 4

Born: Eric Allandale, *Foundations*   Bobby Womack (1948)
(1936)   Chris Rea (1951)
Ron Carter [jazz bassist] (1937)   Ray "Boom Boom" Mancini
Chris Squire, *Yes* (1948)   [World Lightweight Champ]
Jason Newsted, Metallica (1963)   (1961)

Events: The first Congress convenes (1789).

Greta Garbo's first talkie, *Anna Christie,* premieres (1930).

March 5

Born: Rex Harrison (1908)   Andy Gibb (1958)
Samantha Eggar (1939)

Died: Joseph Stalin (1953)   John Belushi [drug overdose]
Jay Silverheels [Tonto on   (1982)
TV's "Lone Ranger" (1980)

Events: Director John Ford receives his first Oscar for *The Informer* (1936).

Elvis is honorably discharged from the army (1960).

"The Stranger" world tour for Billy Joel opens in Holland (1978).

March 6

Born:
Michelangelo (1475)
Furry Lewis [father of the blues] (1893)
Ed McMahon (1923)
Doug Dillard (1937)
Mary Wilson, *The Supremes* (1944)
Randy Meisner (1945)
Hugh Grundy, *The Zombies* (1945)
Kiki Dee (1947)
David Gilmour, *Pink Floyd* (1947)

Events:
The Alamo falls (1836).

Charles Manson releases an LP, "Lies," to finance the Sharon Tate murder trial defense (1970).

The first Women's Lib demonstration is held in London (1971).

March 7

Born:
King Curtis (1934)
Chris White, *The Zombies* (1943)
Matt Fisher, *Procol Harum* (1946)
Peter Wolf, *The J. Geils Band* (1946)

Events:
U.S. Patent No. 174456 is given to Alexander Graham Bell on an invention called the telephone (1876).

The first jazz record, "The Dixie Jazz Band One-Step," is released (1917).

Transatlantic radio telephone is established (1926).

"Dead Man's Curve" by *Jan and Dean* charts (1964).

"Needles and Pins," the first by *The Searchers,* charts (1964).

Michael Jackson becomes the first artist in the history of *Billboard Magazine* charts to simultaneously have the No. 1 slot in Rock LP and single and R & B LP and single — fulfilling the legendary Grand Slam dream (1983).

Richard Thomas portrays Hank Williams, Jr., in a network TV movie (1983).

March 8

Born: Oliver Wendell Holmes (1841)   Lynn Redgrave (1943)
Mississippi John Hurt (1892)   Keith Jarrett (1945)
Jim Bouten (1939)   Gary Numan (1958)

Died: Ron "Pig Pen" McKernan, *The Grateful Dead* (1973).

Events: "Good Golly Miss Molly" by Little Richard charts (1958).

"Aquarius/Let The Sun Shine In" by *The Fifth Dimension* charts (1969).

Joe Frazier defeats Muhammad Ali in the "fight of the century" at Madison Square Garden (1971).

Paul McCartney is fined $100 for growing cannabis on his Scottish farm (1973).

March 9

Born: Amerigo Vespucci (1451)   Mark Lindsay, *Paul Revere and*
Lloyd Price (1933)   *The Raiders* (1944)
Bobby Fischer [ex-world chess   Robin Trower (1945)
champion] (1943)   Jimmy Fadden, *The Dirt Band*
Mickey Dolenz, *The Monkees*   (1948)
(1943)   Trevor Burton, *Move* (1949)

Events: "Monday, Monday" by *The Mamas and the Papas* charts (1966).

CBS-TV cancels "The Smothers Brothers Show," following the brothers' refusal to censor Joan Baez when she dedicated a song to her husband David, who was about to go to jail for his opposition to the draft during the Vietnam war (1969).

March 10

Born: Bix Biederbecke (1903)   Tom Scholz, *Boston* (1947)
Dean Torrance, *Jan and Dean*   Ted McKenna, *The Alex*
(1940)   *Harvey Band* (1950)

Died: Mrs. F. Scott (Zelda Sayre) Fitzgerald (1948).
Andy Gibb (1988)

March 11

Born: Mike Hugg, *Manfred Mann*   Harvey Mandel (1945)
(1940)   Mark Stein, *Vanilla Fudge* (1947)

Died: Johnny Appleseed (1845)

Events: The first *Van Halen* LP is released (1978).

March 12

Born: Edward Albee (1928)
Al Jarreau (1940)
Paul Kantner, *Jefferson Starship* (1942)
Liza Minelli (1946)

James Taylor (1948)
Bill Payne, *Little Feat* (1949)
LaBamba (Richard Rosenberg), ex-*Asbury Jukes* (1953)

Died: Charlie "Bird" Parker [drug-related conditions] (1955)

Events: The Girl Scouts is founded (1912).

"Runaway," Del Shannon's first, makes the charts (1961).

"Good Lovin'" by *The Rascals* charts (1966).

Paul McCartney and Linda Eastman wed (1969).

March 13

Born: Mike Stoller [songwriter] (1933)
Neil Sedaka (1939)

Donald York, *Sha Na Na* (1949)
Adam Clayton, *U-2* (1960)

Events: The planet Uranus is discovered (1781).

Standard time is established (1884).

"Tired of Waiting For You" by *The Kinks* charts (1965).

The first *Van Halen* tour starts in Aragon, Chicago (1978).

March 14

Born: Albert Einstein (1879)

Quincy Jones (1933)

Died: Karl Marx (1883)

Events: The cotton gin is patented (1793).

The first RIAA gold record, "Catch a Falling Star," is awarded to Perry Como (1958).

The Beatles' "Yellow Submarine" album becomes their fourteenth gold LP (1969).

The Stones retire for the first time after a concert in the United Kingdom (1971).

March 15

Born:
Andrew Jackson (1767)
Lightning Hopkins (1912)
Harry James (1916)
Eddie Arnold (1918)
Arif Mardin [producer] (1932)
Phil Lesh, *The Grateful Dead* (1940)

Mike Love, *The Beach Boys* (1941)
Hughie Flint, *McGinnis-Flint* (1942)
Ralph MacDonald (1944)
Sly Stone (1944)
Ry Cooder (1947)

Died:	Julius Caesar (44 B.C.)

Events:	*Pearlie* opens on Broadway (1970).

March 16

Born:
James Madison (1751)
Jerry Lewis (1926)

Jerry Jeff Walker (1942)
Nancy Wilson, *Heart* (1954)

Died:	Tammi Terrell (1970)

Events:	West Point is established (1802).

"Can't Buy Me Love" by *The Beatles* is released (1964).

The New Opry House opens at $15 million cost and is dedicated by President Richard M. Nixon (1974).

Elvis Costello calls Ray Charles and Americans in general a "bunch of niggers." Bonnie Bramlett, drinking with Stephen Stills in the Holiday Inn Lounge in Columbus, Ohio, takes offense, and punches Costello in the face with her fist (1979).

March 17

Born:
Nat "King" Cole (1919)
Rudolf Nureyev (1938)

John Sebastian (1944)
Harold Broan, *War* (1946)

Events:	The first news film is shot, a fire in New York's Windsor Hotel (1899).
Ricki Lee Jones releases her first LP (1979).

March 18

Born:
Grover Cleveland (1837)
Edgar Cayce (1877)
George Plimpton (1927)

Peter Graves (1936)
Wilson Pickett (1941)

Events:
Howard Hughes buys RKO Pictures for $23 million, thus becoming the only sole owner of a movie company (1954).

The Rolling Stones are busted for the first time in Essex, England for public urination (1965).

"Somebody To Love," by The Jefferson Airplane, charts (1967).

California Jam II is held and 250,000 attend (1978).

Teddy Pendergrass crashes his Rolls Royce into a tree. He survives, but loses the use of his legs (1982).

March 19

Born:
Wyatt Earp (1848)
Judge John Sirica (1904)
Ornette Coleman (1930)
Jeff Neighbor, Joy of Cooking (1942)
Ross Valory, Journey (1942)

Paul Atkinson, The Zombies (1943)
Derek Longmuir, Bay City Rollers (1955)
Terry Hill, Specials (1959)

Died:
Paul Kossoff, Free (1976)

Events:
The film South Pacific opens (1958).

"Paradise Theatre" by Styx goes gold (1981).

March 20

Born:
Henrik Ibsen (1828)
Sergei Rachmaninoff (1873)
John Ehrlichman (1925)
Jimmie Vaughan (1951)

Jerry Reed (1937)
Carl Palmer, Asia (1947)
John Wetton, Asia (1951)

Events:
John Lennon and Yoko Ono marry (1969).

David and Angela Bowie marry (1970).

Patty Hearst is found guilty of armed robbery (1976).

March 21

Born: Johann Sebastian Bach (1685)
Florenz Siegfeld (1869)
Sun House (1902)
Maurice Stans (1908)
James Coco (1920)

Eddie Money (1949)
Peter Banks, *Genesis* (1950)
Roger Hodgson, *Supertramp*
(1950)

Events: The Pilgrims and Indians make a treaty (1621).

Allan Freed hosts the first rock show, "Moondog Ball," in Cleveland. He sells 18,000 advance tickets for a 10,000-seat hall. Riots in the streets result (1952).

The Beatles debut at The Cavern Club (1961).

John and Yoko Lennon begin their honeymoon for peace with a week in bed at the Amsterdam Hilton (1969).

Rubin "Hurricane" Carter is released from jail for retrial, thanks to the efforts of Bob Dylan, Muhammad Ali, and others (1976).

March 22

Born: Chico Marx (1887)
Karl "What Will You Do?"
    Malden (1913)
Marcel Marceau (1923)
Keith Relf, *The Yardbirds* (1943)
Jeremy Clyde, *Chad and
    Jeremy* (1944)

Harry Vonda, *Flash In The Pan*
(1947)
Randy Hobbs, *The Johnny
    Winter Band* (1948)

March 23

Born: Joan Crawford (1905)

Events: Patrick Henry delivers his "Give me liberty or give me death" speech in Williamsburg, Virginia (1775).

John Lennon publishes his first book, *In His Own Write* (1964).

March 24

Born: Harry Houdini (1874)
Thomas E. Dewey (1902)
Steve McQueen (1930)

Mike Kellie, *Spooky Tooth*
(1947)
Lee Oskar (1948)

Events: Elvis is inducted into the Army, no. 533 10761 (1958).

Lou Reed, onstage in Buffalo, N.Y., is attacked by a fan who screams "Leather" and bites him on the rear end (1973).

March 25

Born: Ralph Waldo Emerson (1803)   Aretha Franklin (1942)
Howard Cosell (1920)   Elton John (1947)
Johnny Burnette (1934)   Nick Lowe (1949)
Gloria Steinem (1935)

Events: The first concert in New York City by *The Who* takes place (1967).

"Werewolves of London" by Warren Zevon charts (1968).

March 26

Born: Robert Frost (1874)   Diana Ross (1944)
Tennessee Williams (1911)   Richard Tandy, *ELO* (1948)
Alan Arkin (1934)   Steven Tyler, *Aerosmith* (1948)
Fred Paris, *Five Satins* (1936)   Fran Sheehan, *Boston* (1949)

Died: Noel Coward (1973)

Events: *Funny Girl* opens on Broadway starring Barbra Streisand (1964).

Eye, the attempt at a rock magazine by the Hearst Corp., folds (1969).

Gilda Radner and G. Smith wed (1980).

March 27

Born: Gloria Swanson (1899)   Michael York (1942)
Sarah Vaughan (1924)   Wally Stocker, *The Babys* (1949)

Events: "I Can't Explain" is *The Who*'s first hit (1965).

March 28

Born: Edmund Muskie (1914)   John Evans, *Jethro Tull* (1948)
Rufus Thomas (1917)

Died: Arthur "Big Boy" Crudup [heart attack] (1956).

Events: "Long Tall Sally" by Little Richard charts (1956).

The first British pirate radio, Radio Caroline, broadcasts (1964).

The incidents at Three Mile Island startle the country (1979).

Eric Clapton and mentor Muddy Waters' tour starts in Tucson (1979).

David Crosby is arrested for possessing coke, ludes, and a .45 pistol (1982).

March 29

Born:
John Tyler (1790)
Eugene McCarthy (1916)
Pearl Bailey (1918)
Vangelis [Papathanasiou] (1943)
Walt Frazier (1945)
Michael Brecker (1949)

Events: Royal Albert Hall is opened in London by Queen Victoria (1871).

March 30

Born:
Vincent Van Gogh (1853)
Sonny Boy Williamson
  [bluesharp player] (1914)
Warren Beatty (1938)
Graeme Edge, *The Moody Blues* (1944)
Eric Clapton (1945)
Jim Dandy, *Black Oak Arkansas* (1948)
Dave Ball, *Procol Harum* (1948)

Events: Alaska is purchased (1867).

Simon and Garfunkel make their first New York appearance at Gerde's Folk City (1964).

March 31

Born:
Arthur Godfrey (1903)
John D. Loudermilk (1934)
Shirley Jones (1934)
Herb Alpert (1935)
Richard Chamberlin (1935)
Thijs Van Leer, *Focus* (1948)
Mick Ralphs, *Bad Company* (1948)
Richard Hughes, *The Johnny Winter Band* (1950)

Events: Jimi Hendrix burns his guitar on stage for the first time in London (1967).

Muhammad Ali defeats Ken Norton in twelve rounds for the heavyweight title. Norton broke Ali's jaw (1973).

*Herbie
Hancock*

*John
Kay*

*Rick
Allen*

*Kris
Kristofferson*

34

APRIL

April 1

Born: Lon Chaney (1883)
Alberta Hunter (1895)
Willie Dixon (1915)
Debbie Reynolds (1932)

Ali McGraw (1939)
Rudolph Isley (1939)
Ronnie Lane, *Small Faces* (1946)
Arthur Conley (1946)

Died: Scott Joplin, impoverished (1917)

Events: The combustion engine is patented (1826).
David Bowie's first single, "Anything You Say," is released (1966).
Jimi Hendrix's "Are You Experienced" is released (1966).
The Beach Boys sue Capitol Records for $2,041,446.64 (1969).

April 2

Born: Charlemagne (742)
Casanova (1725)
Marvin Gaye (1939)
Leon Russell (1941)

Larry Coryell (1943)
Kerry Minnear, *Gentle Giant* (1948)

Events: The United States Mint is established (1792).
The first movie house opens in Los Angeles featuring *The Capture of The Biddle Brothers*. Admission is 10¢ (1902).

April 3

Born: Washington Irving (1783)
Doris Day (1924)
Marlon Brando (1924)
Johnny Horton (1929)
Jeff Barry [writer] (1939)
Jan Berry, *Jan and Dean* (1941)
Richard Manuel, *The Band* (1943)

Tony Orlando (1944)
Dee Murray, ex-*Elton John Band* (1946)
Richard Thompson (1949)
Mel Schacher, *Grand Funk Railroad* (1951)
Sebastian Bach, Skid Row (1968)
Mick Mars, Motley Crue (1956)

Died: Richard Manuel, *The Band* (1986)

Events: The Pony Express completes its first successful run (1860).
Jesse James is shot (1882).
Billy Preston signs a contract with Apple Records; George Harrison is to produce (1970).
The Cher ABC-TV special with Rod Stewart and *The Tubes* airs (1978).

April 4

Born: Muddy Waters [McKinley Morganfield] (1915)
Major Lance (1941)
Berry Oakley, *The Allman Brothers* (1948)
Pick Withers, *Dire Straits* (1948)
Dave Hill, *Slade* (1952)

Died: Dr. Martin Luther King [assassinated] (1968)

Kurt Weill [composer] (1950)

Events: The United States Congress adopts the flag (1818).

The *Genesis* "Then There Were Three" tour opens in Michigan (1978).

April 5

Born: Booker T. Washington (1856)
Spencer Tracy (1900)
Bette Davis (1908)
Gregory Peck (1916)
Tommy Williams, *The Platters* (1928)
Dave Swarbrick, *Fairport Convention* (1941)
David LaFlamme (1941)
Allan Clarke, *The Hollies* (1942)
Anna Ulvaeus, *Abba* (1950)
Julian Lennon (1963)

Died: Bob "Bear" Hite [heart attack] (1981)

April 6

Born: Lowell Thomas (1892)
Merle Haggard (1937)
Michelle Phillips, *The Mamas and the Papas* (1944)
Bob Marley (1946)

Died: Howard Hughes (1976)

Events: *The Rolling Stones* sign a distribution deal with Atlantic Records (1971).

April 7

Born: Billie Holiday (1915)
Percy Faith (1918)
Ravi Shankar (1920)
Charley Thomas, *The Drifters* (1937)
Spencer Dryden, *New Riders of the Purple Sage* (1938)
Freddie Hubbard (1938)
David Frost (1939)
Mick Abrams, *Jethro Tull* (1943)
John Oates, *Hall and Oates* (1949)
Janis Ian (1951)

Died: P. T. Barnum (1891)

Events: Steve Winwood's "Arc of a Diver" goes gold (1981).

April 8

Born: Mary Pickford (1893)   Steve Howe, *Asia* (1947)
              Jacques Brel (1929)   Julian Lennon [John and
                                            Cynthia's son] (1963)

Died: Pablo Picasso (1973)

Events: *Time* magazine asks, "Is God Dead?" (1966).

              The Grateful Dead release their first LP (1967).

              Neil Young's *Journey Through The Past* film premieres in Dallas (1973).

              "London Town" by *Wings* is released (1978).

April 9

Born: W. C. Fields (1879)   Gene Parsons, *The Byrds* (1944)
              Hugh Hefner (1926)   Steve Gadd (1949)
              Carl Perkins (1932)   Chico Ryan, *Sha Na Na* (1948)
              Terry Knight (1943)
              Izzy Stradlin, ex-Guns N' Roses (1962)

Died: Phil Ochs [folksinger; hung himself] (1976).

Events: The Civil War ends (1865).

              Sir Winston Churchill is made an honorary United States citizen (1963).

              "Ticket to Ride" by *The Beatles* is released (1965).

              The Houston Astrodome opens (1965).

              "Eight Miles High" by *The Byrds* charts (1966).

April 10

Born: Sheb Wooley [Purple People   Arthur Ashe (1943)
                 Eater] (1921)   Bunny Wailer (1947)
              Omar Sharif (1933)   Dave Peverett, *Foghat* (1950)
              Glen Campbell (1936)   Terre Roche, *The Roches* (1953)
              Bobby Hatfield, *The Righteous*
                 Brothers (1940)

Died: Stu Sutcliffe [would have been a Beatle] (1962).

Events: *The Titanic* leaves on its maiden voyage (1912).

              Nat King Cole is badly beaten onstage by a white anti-rhythm and
              blues crowd (1956).

April 11

Born: Ethel Kennedy (1928)   Robbie House, *Snuff* (1951)
Joel Grey (1932)

Events: Eddie Van Halen and Valerie Bertinelli wed (1981).

April 12

Born: Tiny Tim (1930)   David Cassidy (1950)
Herbie Hancock (1940)   Pat Travers (1954)
John Kay, *Steppenwolf* (1944)

Events: *Bill Haley and The Comets* record "Rock Around The Clock" (1954).

Jan Berry, of *Jan and Dean,* hits dead man's curve in his 'Vette. His lower body and speech are paralyzed for five years (1966).

The first flight of United States spaceship *Columbia* (1981).

April 13

Born: Thomas Jefferson (1743)   Roy Loney, *Flaming Groovies*
F. W. Woolworth (1852)   (1946)
Lester Chambers, *Chambers*   Jim Pons, *Mothers of Invention*
Brothers (1940)   (1946)
Eve Graham, *New Seekers*   Max Weinberg, *E Street Band*
(1943)   (1951)
Jack Casady, *Hot Tuna* (1944)   Jimmy Destri, *Blondie* (1954)
Al Green (1946)

Events: Roger Daltrey releases his first solo LP (1973).

April 14

Born: Rod Steiger (1925)   Ritchie Blackmore, *Rainbow*
Loretta "Coal Miner's   (1945)
Daughter" Lynn (1940)

Events: *Bye Bye Birdie* opens on Broadway (1960).

April 15

Born: Bessie Smith (1898)   Dave Edmunds (1944)
Henry James (1843)

Events: *The Titanic* sinks; 513 lives are lost at sea (1912).

Elvis Costello's "This Year's Model" is released (1978).

Billy Joel nearly dies in a motorcycle crash (1982).

April 16

Born: Wilbur Wright [inventor of the airplane] (1867)
Charlie Chaplin (1889)
Peter Ustinov (1921)
Henry Mancini (1924)
Herbie Mann (1930)
Dusty Springfield (1939)
Bobby Vinton (1946)

Events: "Brown Sugar" is the first single on *The Stones'* own label (1971).

April 17

Born: Thornton Wilder (1897)
Nikolai Krushchev (1894)
William Holden (1918)
Harry Reasoner (1923)
Don Kirshner (1934)
Roy Estrada, *Mothers of Invention* (1943)
Jan Hammer (1948)

Died: Ben Franklin (1790)
Eddie Cochran [car crash] (1960)
Vinnie Taylor, *Canned Heat* [drug overdose] (1974)

Events: Johnny Cash plays at the White House for Richard Nixon (1970).

April 18

Born: Mike Vickers, *Manfred Mann* (1941)
Lenny Baker, *Sha Na Na* (1946)

Events: Paul Revere makes his famous ride (1775).

April 19

Born: Alexis Korner (1928)
Jayne Mansfield (1933)
Alan Price, *The Animals* (1942)
Mark Volman, *Flo and Eddie* (1947)

Died: Albert Einstein (1955)
Alfred Hitchcock (1980)

Events: Grace Kelly marries Prince Rainier and becomes the first United States citizen to marry a reigning monarch (1956).

"Johnny B. Goode" by Chuck Berry charts (1958).

April 20

Born: Mohammed (570)   Johnny Tillotson (1939)
             Napoleon (1808)   Craig Frost, *Grand Funk*
             Harold Lloyd (1894)   *Railroad* (1948)

Events: "Your Hit Parade" debuts on radio (1935).

             Family Affair, the first of seventeen Andy Hardy movies, opens star-
             ring Mickey Rooney (1937).

April 21

Born: Anthony Quinn (1914)   Alan Warner, *The Foundations*
             Queen Elizabeth II (1926)   (1947)
             Iggy Pop (1947)   Paul Davis (1948)

Events: The Seattle World's Fair opens (1962).

             Annie opens on Broadway (1977).

             "Heart of Glass" by *Blondie* becomes the first New Wave song to top
             the charts (1979).

April 22

Born: Charles Mingus (1922)   Peter Frampton (1950)

Events: John Lennon changes his name to John Ono Lennon (1969).

             The last American convertible of the decade is made in Detroit; it is a
             Cadillac Eldorado (1976).

             "Kaya" by *Bob Marley and the Wailers* charts (1978).

             "Baker Street" by Gerry Rafferty charts (1978).

             The Rolling Stones play two benefit shows in Toronto to pay for Keith
             Richard's heroin bust (1979).

April 23

Born: William Shakespeare (1564)   Roy Orbison (1936)
             Shirley Temple (1928)   Narada Michael Walden (1952)

Died: William Shakespeare (1616)   Peter Ham, *Badfinger* (1975)

Events: "Dirty Water" by *The Standells* charts (1966).

             "Respect" by Aretha Franklin charts (1967).

April 24

Born: Barbra Streisand (1942)
Stu Cook, *Creedence Clearwater Revival* (1945)

Doug Clifford, *Creedence Clearwater Revival* (1945)
Glen Cornick, *Jethro Tull* (1947)

Events: The Library of Congress is established (1800).

April 25

Born: Guglielmo Marconi [radio inventor] (1874)
Edward R. Murrow (1908)
Ella Fitzgerald (1918)

Albert King [blues guitarist] (1924)
Jerry Leiber [songwriter] (1933)
Al Pacino (1940)
Bjorn Ulvaeus, *Abba* (1945)

Died: Pam Morrison [Jim's wife; of a drug overdose] (1974).

Events: Elvis has his first No. 1 hit, "Heartbreak Hotel" (1956).

April 26

Born: Gertrude "Ma" Rainey (1886)
Carol Burnett (1935)
Maurice Williams (1938)
Duane Eddy (1938)

Bobby Rydell (1942)
Gary Wright (1945)
Pete Ham, *Badfinger* (1947)
Jimmy Hall, *Wet Willie* (1949)

Events: "Kookie, Kookie, Lend Me Your Comb" by Ed "Kookie" Byrnes makes the charts (1959).

April 27

Born: Samuel F. Morse [Morse code] (1781)
Ulysees S. Grant (1822)

Ann Peebles (1947)
Paul "Ace" Frehley, *Kiss* (1951)
Sheena Easton (1959)

Died: Phil King, *Blue Oyster Cult* [shot in head while gambling] (1972).

Events: Ringo and Barbara Bach wed in London (1981).

April 28

Born: James Monroe (1758)   Ann-Margret (1941)
            Lionel Barrymore (1878)   Steve Khan (1947)

Died: Benito Mussolini (1945)

Events: The mutiny on *The Bounty* takes place (1789).

            The Boxing Commission takes the world title from Muhammad Ali
            for his stance on the draft laws (1967).

            Hair opens in New York City (1968).

April 29

Born: William Randolph Hearst (1863)   Rod McKuen (1933)
            Duke Ellington (1899)   Hugh Hopper, *Soft Machine*
            Hirohito (1901)   (1945)
            Carl Gardner, *The Coasters*   Tommy James (1947)
                (1928)

Died: LeRoy Carr (1935)   Marvin Gaye [shot to death by
            Frankie Lymon [drug overdose]   his father] (1984)
                (1968)

Events: Dick Clark testifies to the Senate about payola (1960).

            The Rolling Stones sign with Andrew Loog Oldham to be their man-
            ager (1963).

            "Hey Joe," by Jimi Hendrix, charts (1967).

April 30

Born: Willie Nelson (1933)   Mike Beacon, *Ox* (1945)
            Bobby Vee (1943)

Died: Richard Farina, writer   Lester Bangs [rock critic] (1982)
                [motorcycle accident] (1966)

Events: George Washington is inaugurated as the first president (1789).

            "My Little Red Book" by *Love* is the first hit for Elektra Records (1966).

            Twiggs Lyndon, *The Allman Brothers* road manager, is arrested for
            killing a club owner over a breach of contract (1970).

*David Lee
Roth*

*Hall and
Oates*

*Bon
Jovi*

44

MAY

May 1

Born:　Kate Smith (1909)　　　　　Rudolf Isley (1939)
Glenn Ford (1916)　　　　Judy Collins (1939)
Jack Paar (1918)　　　　　Rita Coolidge (1944)
Little Walter (1930)

Died:　J. Edgar Hoover (1972)

Events:　*Citizen Kane* opens in Radio City Music Hall (1941).

"I'm Walking" becomes Rick Nelson's first hit (1957).

The first United States plane is hijacked to Cuba (1961).

The Beatles and *The Rolling Stones* play the "New Music Express" Readers' Poll concert in Wembley (1966).

Elvis Presley and Priscilla Beaulieu wed (1967).

Bob Dylan and Johnny Cash tape "Grand Ole Opry Special" for ABC-TV (1969)

May 2

Born:　Catherine the Great (1729)　　　Englebert Humperdinck (1936)
Baron Von Richtofen, "The Red　　　Hilton Valentine, *The Animals*
Baron" (1892)　　　　　　　　(1943)
Dr. Benjamin Spock (1903)　　　　John Verity, *Argent* (1944)
Harry Lillis, "Bing" Crosby　　　　Goldy McJohn, *Steppenwolf*
(1904)　　　　　　　　　　　(1945)
Bunk Gardner, *The Mothers of*　　Lesley Gore (1946)
Invention (1933)　　　　　　　Lou Graham, *Foreigner* (1950)
Link Wray (1935)

Died:　Sen. Joseph McCarthy (1957)

May 3

Born: Golda Meir (1898)   Peter Staples (1944)
              Pete Seeger (1919)   Mary Hopkins (1950)
              James Brown (1928)   Steve Jones, *The Sex Pistols*
              Johnny Unitas (1933)   (1955)
              Frankie Valli (1937)   David Ball, *Soft Cell* (1959)

Event: *Meet John Doe* starring Gary Cooper and Barbara Stanwyck
              premieres (1941).

May 4

Born: Audrey Hepburn (1929)   Ronnie Band, *Troggs* (1944)
              Ed Cassidy, *Spirit* (1931)   Zal Cleminson, *The Alex
              Tammy Wynette (1942)   Harvey Band* (1949)

Died: Four students are shot by the National Guard at Kent State Univer-
              sity in an anti-war demonstration (1970).

              Moe (Three Stooges) Howard (1975)

Events: "Be Bop A Lula" is cut by Gene Vincent. He wrote the song on a
              train to compete in an Elvis sound-alike contest (1956).

              Lucy and Desi get their final divorce papers (1960).

May 5

Born: Karl Marx (1818)   Ian McCullough, *Echo and the
              Bill Ward, *Black Sabbath* (1948)   Bunnymen* (1959)

Events: Carnegie Hall opens (1891).

              Alan Shepard becomes the first American in space (1961).

              John F. Kennedy raises the minimum hourly wage from 25¢ to $1.25
              (1961).

              The Buffalo Springfield officially breaks up (1968).

May 6

Born: Sigmund Freud (1865)   Willie Mays (1931)
              Rudolph Valentino (1895)   Herbie Cox, *The
              Orson Welles (1915)   Cleftones* (1939)
              Peggy Lee [Norma Dolores   Bob Seger (1945)
                Estram] (1920)

Events: Rome is sacked, ending the Renaissance (1527).

May 7

Born:

Robert Browning (1812)
Johannes Brahms (1833)
Peter Ilich Tchaikovsky (1840)
Gary Cooper (1901)
Anne Baxter (1923)

Jimmy Ruffin, *The Temptations* (1939)
Johnny Maestro (1939)
Pete Wingfield (1948)
Derek Taylor (1952)

Events:

The Lusitania is torpedoed by a German sub (1915).

World War II ends (1945).

May 8

Born:

Harry Truman (1884)
Don Rickles (1926)
Rick Nelson (1940)
Euclid "Motorhead" Sherwood, *Mothers of Invention* (1942)
Toni Tennille (1943)
Paul Samwell-Smith, *The Yardbirds* (1943)

Gary Glitter [Paul Gadd] (1944)
Candice Bergen (1946)
Marc Bolan, *T Rex* (1947)
Philip Bailey (1951)
Chris Frantz, *Talking Heads* (1951)
Billy Burnette, *Fleetwood Mac* (1953)

Died:

Graham Bond [jumped under train] (1974)

Neil Bogart, producer [of cancer] (1982)

Events:

John S. Pemberton first mixed ingredients for Coca-Cola in Jacob's Pharmacy, Atlanta, Georgia (1886).

V-E [Victory in Europe] Day (1945).

May 9

Born:

Mike Wallace (1918)
Pancho Gonzalez (1928)
Glenda Jackson (1936)
Dave Prater, *Sam and Dave* (1937)
Tommy Roe (1942)

Don Danneman, *Cyrkle* (1944)
Pete Birrell, *Dreamers* (1944)
Richie Furay (1944)
Steve Katz (1945)
Billy Joel (1949)

Events:

Admiral Byrd makes the first flight to the North Pole (1926).

The Food and Drug Administration okays the sale of birth control pills (1960).

Federal Communications Commission Chairman Minow calls TV a "vast wasteland" (1961).

The Beatles sign a contract with EMI's Parlophone Records (1962).

May 10

Born:

Fred Astaire [Frederick
    Austerlitz] (1889)
Danny Rapp, *Danny and the
    Juniors* (1941)
Jackie Lomax (1944)
Donovan P. Leitch (1946)

Dave Mason (1946)
Jay Ferguson (1947)
Sid Vicious, *The Sex Pistols*
    (1957)
Sly "Drumbar" Dunbar (1952)
Bono Vox (Paul Hughson) (1960)

Died:

T. J. "Stonewall" Jackson (1863)

Events:

The Rolling Stones have their first recording session at Olympic
Studios, London (1963).

The Turtles and *The Temptations* play Tricia Nixon's White House
Masque Ball (1969).

The Who sell out four nights in Madison Square Garden (80,000 seats)
in less than eight hours (1974).

May 11

Born:

Irving Berlin (1888)
Salvador Dali (1904)
Phil Silvers (1912)
Mort Sahl (1927)
Doug McClure (1935)

Carla Bley (1938)
Eric Burdon (1941)
Les Chadwick, *Gerry and
    the Pacemakers* (1943)
Martha Quinn, MTV Video Jock

Died:

Lester Flatt (1979)

Bob Marley [cancer] (1981)

Events:

General Electric's New York station, WEY, has the first scheduled
TV broadcast. A spokesman said, "Only the faces of men talking,
laughing, or smoking will be broadcast. No elaborate effects are
planned at this time" (1928).

May 12

Born: Florence Nightingale (1820)   Ian Drury (1942)
            Yogi Berra (1925)   Billy Swan (1944)
            Burt Bacharach (1929)   Ian McLagan, *Faces* (1945)
            George Carlin (1938)   Steve Winwood (1948)
            Ron Zeigler (1939)

Events: Richmond, Virginia falls to the North in the Civil War (1854).

Bob Dylan refuses to play "The Ed Sullivan Show" because he's not allowed to sing "Talking John Birch Society Blues" (1963).

The Stones play the "New Music Express" winner's concert, Wembley (1968).

Pink Floyd presents the first quadrophonic rock concert in Queen Elizabeth Hall, England (1967).

Mick Jagger and Bianca Moreno wed (1971).

Jefferson Starship [Airplane] celebrate their tenth anniversary with a free Central Park concert (1975).

May 13

Born: Joe Louis (1914)   Pete "Overend" Watts, *Mott the*
            Clive Barnes (1927)   *Hoople* (1947)
            Richie Valens (1941)   Stevie [Steveland Morris
            Mary Wells, *The Supremes*   Hardaway] Wonder (1950)
               (1943)   Danny Kirwan, ex-*Fleetwood*
            Magic Dick, *The J. Geils Band*   *Mac* (1950)
               (1945)   Peter Gabriel (1950)

Died: Bob Wills (1975)

Events: Jamestown is settled (1607).

"Groovin'" by *The Rascals* charts (1967).

May 14

Born: Bobby Darin (1936)   David Byrne, *Talking Heads*
            Jack Bruce (1943)   *Heads* (1952)
            Gene Cornish, *The Rascals*
               (1945)

May 15

Born:

Richard Daley (1902)
James Mason (1909)
Joseph Cotten (1905)
Eddie Arnold (1918)

Trini Lopez (1937)
Brian Peter George St. John de
   Baptiste Delafalle Eno (1948)
Mike Oldfield (1953)

Events:

"Bye, Bye Love," the first hit for the Everly Brothers, charts (1957).

Judy Garland's last film opens, *I Could Go On Singing* (1963).

"For Your Love" is *The Yardbirds'* first hit (1965).

"Mr. Tambourine Man" is *The Byrds'* first hit (1965).

May 16

Born:

Studs Terkel (1912)
Woody Herman (1913)
Henry Fonda (1915)
Liberace (1919)
Billy Cobham (1944)

Roger Earl, *Foghat* (1946)
Barbara Lee, *The Chiffons*
   (1947)
Jock Bartley, *Firefall* (1950)
Jonathan Richman (1951)

Events:

Pete Townshend kicks a plainclothes cop offstage in Fillmore East and goes to jail. Bill Graham pays his bail (1969).

The first Academy Awards ceremony is held (1929).

May 17

Born:

Archibald Cox (1912)
Dennis Hopper (1936)
Taj Mahal (1942)
Jesse Winchester (1944)

Bill Bruford, *Genesis* (1950)
"Sugar" Ray [Charles] Leonard
   (1956)

Events:

"Rave On" by Buddy Holly is released (1958).

Don't Look Back, a film about Dylan's United Kingdom tour, opens in San Francisco (1967).

Godspell opens on Broadway (1971).

May 18

Born: Jacob Javitz (1904)   Brooks Robinson (1937)
             Joe Turner (1911)   Rick Wakeman, ex-*Yes* (1949)
             Perry Como (1912)   Wreckless Eric (1954)

Events: Grauman's Chinese Theater opens in Hollywood (1927).

             The Beatles begin their first national United Kingdom tour, headlined
             by Roy Orbison (1963).

             The Me Nobody Knows opens (1970).

             Mt. St. Helens erupts (1980).

May 19

Born: Ho Chi Minh (1890)   Jerry Hyman, *Blood, Sweat,*
             Malcolm X (Little) (1925)   *and Tears* (1947)
             David Hartman (1937)   Tom Scott (1948)
             Peter [Dennis Blandford]   Joey Ramone (1952)
                Townshend (1945)   Grace Jones (1952)

Died: Coleman Hawkins (1969)

May 20

Born: James Stewart (1908)   "Little" Jimmy Henderson,
             Moshe Dayan (1915)   *Black Oak Arkansas* (1954)
             George Gobel (1920)   Nick Heyward, *Haircut 100*
             Vic Ames (1926)   (1961)
             Joe Cocker (1944)   Jane Wiedlin, *The Go-Go's*
             Cher (1945)   (1958)

Events: "Windy" by *The Association* charts (1967).

             Peter Cetera, *Chicago*, gets four teeth knocked out at a Chicago Cubs
             baseball game when three men object to the length of his hair (1971).

             "Rumours" by *Fleetwood Mac* becomes the first million-selling LP in
             Canada (1978).

May 21

Born: Raymond Burr (1917)
Peggy Cass (1936)
Dennis Day (1937)
Ronald Isley (1941)

Hilton Valentine, *The Animals* (1943)
Leo Sayer (1948)

Events: The Red Cross is established (1881).

Charles Lindbergh arrives at LeBouget, Paris from New York City after a 33-1/2-hour solo flight, the first (1927).

"Solitary Man" is Neil Diamond's first hit (1966).

Peter Townshend weds Karen Ashley (1968).

Elton John becomes the first rock act to tour Russia. Tickets are scalped at $150 (1979).

May 22

Born: Sir Arthur Conan Doyle (1859)
Sir Laurence Olivier (1907)
Harry Vanda, *Flash In The Pan* (1947)

Bernie Taupin (1950)
Jarry Dammers, *Specials* (1954)

Events: Bob Dylan has his bar mitzvah (1954).

Lyndon B. Johnson introduces the term "The Great Society" (1964).

May 23

Born: Douglas Fairbanks (1883)
Artie Shaw (1910)
Bumps Blackwell (1918)
Robert A. Moog [inventor of synthesizer] (1934)

General George Norman Johnson, *Chairmen of the Board* (1943)

Died: Kit Carson (1868)

Elmore James (1963)

Events: The film *Annie Get Your Gun* opens (1950).

The Grateful Dead play their first United Kingdom concert (1970).

Clive Davis is fired as president of CBS Records (1973).

May 24

Born: Queen Victoria (1819)
Bob Dylan [Robert Allen
Zimmerman] (1941)

Patti LaBelle (1944)
Steve Upton, *Wishbone Ash*
(1946)

Died: Duke Ellington (1974)

Events: Manhattan is bought from the Indians for $24 in beads (1626).

May 25

Born: Ralph Waldo Emerson (1803)
Gene Tierney (1897)
Hal David (1921)
Miles Davis (1926)

Tom T. Hall (1936)
Leslie Uggams (1943)
Poli Palmer, *Family* (1943)
Jessi Colter (1947)

Died: Sonny Boy Williamson (1965)

May 26

Born: Al Jolson (1886)
John Wayne [Marion Morrison]
(1908)
Robert Morley (1908)
James Arness (1923)

Jackie Liebesit, *Can* (1938)
Levon Helm, *The Band* (1942)
Verden "Phally" Allen, *Mott the
Hoople* (1944)
Stevie Nicks (1948)

Events: John and Yoko start a "Bed-In For Peace" and record "Give Peace A
Chance" in their room at the Queen Elizabeth Hotel in Montreal (1969).

May 27

Born: Dashiell Hammett (1894)
Vincent Price (1911)
Hubert H. Humphrey (1911)
John F. Kennedy (1917)

Henry Kissinger (1923)
Ramsey Lewis (1935)
Cilla Black (1943)

Events: "That'll Be The Day" is the first *Crickets'* record with Buddy Holly
(1957).

"Miss You" by *The Rolling Stones* charts (1978).

May 28-30

Events: U.S. Festival 1983 (400,000) (1983).

May 28

Born: T-Bone Walker (1910)   Gladys Knight (1944)
Papa John Creech, *Hot Tuna*   John Fogerty, *Creedence*
  (1917)   *Clearwater Revival* (1945)
Carroll Baker (1931)

Events: The first full-color talkie opens at the Wintergarden Theater in New York City (1929).

"Quarter to 3" by Gary U.S. Bonds charts (1961).

May 29

Born: Patrick Henry (1736)   Mike Rossi, *Status Quo* (1945)
Bob Hope (1903)   Gary Brooker, *Procol Harum*
Irmin Schmidt, *Can* (1937)   (1945)
Roy Crewsdon, *The Dreamers*
  (1941)

Events: Roger McGuinn gives his first post-*Byrds* concert at the Academy of Music (1973).

Bruce Springsteen plays in London for the first time since 1975 (1981).

May 30

Born: Benny Goodman (1909)   Nicky Headon, *The Clash*
Lenny Davidson, *The Dave*   (1955)
  Clark Five (1942)

Died: Tommy Caldwell, *The Marshall Tucker Band* (1980)

Events: "Memphis" becomes Johnny Rivers' first hit (1964).

May 31

Born: Walt Whitman (1819)   Joe Namath (1943)
Prince Rainier III (1923)   Mick Ralphs, *Bad Company*
Clint Eastwood (1930)   (1944)
Peter Yarrow (1938)   John Bonham, *Led Zeppelin*
Augie Mayer, *Sir Douglas*   (1948)
  Quintet (1940)

Van
Morrison

Eric
Clapton

55

*Muddy
Waters*

*Merle
Haggard*

JUNE

June 1

Born:
Nelson Riddle (1921)
Marilyn Monroe (1926)
Andy Griffith (1926)
Pat Boone (1934)

Ron Wood, *The Rolling Stones* (1947)
Tom Robinson

Died: Sonny Boy Williamson (1948)

Events: The first Superman comic is released (1938).

The Rolling Stones start their first United States tour (1964).

"Sergeant Pepper" is released in the United Kingdom (1967).

"Dark Side of the Moon" by *Pink Floyd* is released in Ultra High Quality Recording in 5,000 quantity, the ultimate pressing ever by Mobile Fidelity (1981).

June 2

Born:
Charlie Watts (1941)
William Guest, *Pips* (1941)

Tony Hadley, *Spandau Ballet* (1959)

Events: Glen Matlock (bass) is ejected from *The Sex Pistols* for liking *The Beatles* (1980).

The Pretenders LP goes gold (1980).

June 3

Born:
Jefferson David (1808)
Josephine Baker (1906)
Tony Curtis (1925)
Allen Ginsburg [poet] (1926)
Curtis Mayfield (1942)

Michael Clarke, *Firefall* (1944)
Ian Hunter (1946)
Suzie Quatro (1950)
Dan Hill (1954)

Died: Ralph Gleason [co-founder of *Rolling Stone*] (1975).

Events: *The Rolling Stones* make their United States TV debut on "The Dean Martin Show (1964).

Ed White of *Gemini Four* makes the first space walk (1965).

June 4

Born: Gordon Waller, *Peter and Gordon* (1945)

Died: Murray Wilson, father of three *Beach Boys* (1973).

Events: "Hanky Panky" becomes Tommy James' first hit (1966).

The first rock royalties paid from Russia are to *The Rolling Stones* (1975).

June 5

Born: Bill Hayes ["Ballad of Davy Crockett"] (1926)

Michael Monarch, *Steppenwolf* (1946)

Died: Robert Kennedy [assassinated] (1968)

Events: Ben Franklin discovers electricity with the kite, key, and storm method (1752).

Bob Dylan graduates from Hibbing High School, Minnesota (1959).

June 6

Born: Nathan Hale (1755)
Gary U. S. Bonds (1936)
Larry "The Mole" Taylor, *Canned Heat* (1942)

Edgar Froese, *Tangerine Dream* (1944)
Peter Albin, *Big Brother and the Holding Company* (1944)

Events: "Ooby Dooby," Roy Orbison's first hit, charts (1956).

Elvis appears on "The Ed Sullivan Show" from the waist up (1956).

The Beatles begin their first session with EMI, at Abbey Road Studios, with George Martin as producer (1962).

June 7

Born: Dean Martin (1917)
Rocky Graziano (1922)
Tom Jones (1940)
Clarence White, *The Byrds* (1944)

Bill Kreutzmann, *The Grateful Dead* (1946)
Prince [Prince Rogers Nelson] (1960)

Died: Claudette Orbison [Roy's wife, in a motorcycle accident] (1966).

Events: The YMCA is nationally established (1854).

The Rolling Stones make their first TV appearance on "Thank Your Lucky Stars" (1963).

Blind Faith appears for the first time in public at London's Hyde Park for 150,000 fans (1969).

The Bob Dylan and Johnny Cash TV special airs on ABC (1969).

June 8

Born:
Nancy Sinatra (1940)
Chuck Negron, *Three Dog Night* (1942)
Boz Scaggs (1944)

Julie Driscoll (1947)
Mick Box, *Uriah Heep* (1947)
Alex Van Halen (1950)
Nick Rhodes, *Duran Duran* (1962)

Died:
Laverne Andrews (1967)

Jimmy Rushing (1972)

Events:
Bob Dylan records and hour-long BBC-TV special (1965).

Brian Jones announces his departure from *The Rolling Stones* (1969).

June 9

Born:
Cole Porter (1893)
Les Paul (1923)
Johnny Ace (1929)
Jackie Wilson (1934)

Jon Lord, *Deep Purple* (1941)
Mitch Mitchell, *The Jimi Hendrix Experience* (1947)

Events:
The Beatles begin their first tour of the Orient and Hong Kong (1964).
Bob Dylan receives an honorary degree from Princeton (1970).

Elvis plays New York City for the first time (1972).

Bruce Springsteen signs with CBS records (1972).

June 10

Born:
Howlin' Wolf [Chester Burnett] (1910)
Prince Philip (1921)
Judy Garland (1922)
Maurice Sendak (1928)

Maurice Sendak (1928)
Rick Price, *Move* (1944)
Matthew Fischer, *Procol Harum* (1946)

Events:
Janis Joplin plays with *Big Brother and the Holding Company* for the first time (1966).

The Beatles release "Rain," the first recording with reversed tapes (1966).

Bruce Springsteen releases "Darkness On The Edge of Town" (1978).

Richard Pryor is severely burned while either using freebase coke or eating chocolate chip cookies and milk (1980).

June 11

Born:
Jacques Cousteau (1910)
Pinetop Smith (1914)

Chad Everett (1936)

Died:
John Wayne (1979)

Events:
Chuck Berry pleads guilty to income tax evasion (1979).

June 12

Born:

Jim Nabors (1933)
Roy Harper (1941)
Chick Corea (1941)
Len Barry, *The Dovells* (1942)
Reg Presley, *The Troggs* (1943)

Archie Bleyer (1949)
Brad Delp, *Boston* (1951)
Bun E. Carols, *Cheap Trick* (1951)
Rocky Burnette (1953)

Died: Jimmy Dorsey (1957)

Events: New York City incorporates (1665).

The Beatles receive the MBE (Member of British Empire) award for "Services to Export." Several quite-right members resign in protest (1965).

The Who's movie, *The Kids Are Alright,* opens (1979).

Bruce Springsteen, Jackson Browne, Linda Ronstadt, etc., host a nuclear disarmament rally in Central Park; 750,000 attend (1982).

June 13

Born:

Basil Rathbone (1892)
Red Grange (1904)
Bobby Freeman (1940)

Dennis Locorriere,
Dr. Hook (1949)
Jorge Santana, *Malo* (1954)

Died: Clyde McPhatter, *The Drifters* (1972).

Events: Frank Zappa graduates from Antelope Valley High School, Lancaster, California (1958).

June 14

Born:

Burl Icle Ivanhoe Ives (1909)
Gene Barry (1922)
Che Guevara (1928)

Muff Winwood, *Spencer Davis Group* (1943)
Rod Argent (1945)

Events: *The Rolling Stones* announce the formation of their own label (1969).

June 15

Born:

Errol Garner (1921)
Harry Nilsson (1941)

Waylon Jennings (1947)
Noddy Holder, *Slade* (1950)

Events: Ivan Vaughan introduces a drunk John Lennon to a sober Paul McCartney (1956).

"Surf City" by *Jan and Dean* charts (1963).

The Beatles release the original "butcher" cover of "Yesterday and Today" (1966).

June 16

Born: Katherine Graham (1917)   Gino Vanelli (1952)
Erich Segal (1937)   Gary Roberts, *Boomtown Rats*
Lamont Dozier (1941)   (1954)

Died: James Honeywell-Scott, *The Pretenders* [drug overdose] (1982).

Events: *Psycho* opens in Hollywood (1960).

Rudolf Nureyev defects from Russia at the Paris airport (1961).

The Monterey Pop Festival opens (1967).

June 17

Born: Igor Stravinsky (1882)   Chris Spedding (1944)
M. C. Escher (1898)   Barry Manilow (1944)
Lena Horne (1917)   Boy George (1961)
Dickie Do [& The Don'ts) (1939)

Events: Russia's Valentina Tereshkova becomes the first woman in outer space (1963).

Moby Grape releases five simultaneous singles in their CBS debut (1967).

June 18

Born: Jeanette McDonald (1907)   James Paul McCartney (1942)
E. G. Marshall (1910)   Cyndi Lauper (1953)
Richard Boone (1916)   Dizzy Reed, Guns N' Roses

Events: The Battle of Waterloo occurs outside Brussels (1815).

June 19

Born: Guy Lombardo (1902)   Al Wilson (1939)
Lou Gehrig (1903)   Spanky McFarlane (1942)
Tommy DeVito, *The Four*   Ann Wilson, *Heart* (1950)
Seasons (1935)

Events: The first nickelodeon opens in Pittsburgh (1905).

"Whole Lotta Shakin'" is Jerry Lee Lewis' explosion into rock (1957).

June 20

Born:
Errol Flynn (1909)
Chet Atkins (1924)
Brian Wilson (1942)
Anne Murray (1946)
Nigel Morris, *Isotope* (1948)
Alan Longmuir, *Bay City Rollers* (1953)

Michael Anthony, *Van Halen* (1955)
John Taylor, *Duran Duran* (1960)

Events:
The United States Congress adapts the Great Seal (1782).

Abbott & Costello's "Who's On First" is first seen in *Naughty 90's* film (1945).

The Newport Folk Festival draws 150,000 people (1969).

June 21

Born:
Alexander the Great (356 B.C.)
Martha Washington (1731)
O. C. Smith (1936)
Ray Davies, *Kinks* (1944)
Chris Britton, *The Troggs* (1945)

Joey Cramer, *Aerosmith* (1950)
William Arthur Louis [Prince Charles and Princess Diana's son] (1982)

Events:
Dr. Peter Goldmark of CBS Records demonstrates the first 33-1/3 RPM long-playing record (1948).

Donald Fagen and Walter Becker formally dissolve *Steely Dan* (1981).

June 22

Born:
John Dillinger (1903)
Joseph Papp (1921)
Bill Blass (1922)
Kris Kristofferson (1936)

Peter Asher (1946)
Howard Kaylan, *Flo and Eddie* (1945)
Todd Rundgren (1948)

Events:
The saxophone is patented by Adolphe Sax (1846).

"Wipe Out" by *The Surfaris* charts (1963).

June 23

Born:
Bob Fosse (1927)

June Carter (1929)

Events:
John Entwistle weds Alison Wise (1967).

Lyndon B. Johnson and Kosygin meet at Glassboro, NJ (1967).

Smokey Robinson and the Miracles perform their last show together (1972).

June 24

Born: Jack Dempsey (1895)
Memphis Minnie (1900)
Jeff Beck (1944)
Arthur Brown (1944)

Chris Wood, *Traffic* (1944)
Colin Blunstone, *The Zombies* (1945)
Mick Fleetwood (1947)

Events: The first million-dollar movie contract is awarded to Mary Pickford for two years (1916).

John Lennon's second book, *A Spaniard in the Works,* is published (1965).

"Purple Haze" by Jimi Hendrix charts (1967).

"White Rabbit" by *Jefferson Airplane* charts (1967).

June 25

Born: George Orwell (1903)
Eddie Floyd (1935)
Carly Simon (1945)

Clint Warwick [ex-*Moody Blues*] (1949)
Ian McDonald, *Foreigner* (1946)

Events: Custer's last stand at Little Big Horn (1876).

The first film with sound effects, *Old San Francisco,* is released (1927).

Billboard changes the name of "race" charts to :"rhythm & blues" charts (1949).

June 26

Born: Big Bill Broonzy (1893)
Peter Lorre (1904)
Colonel Tom Parker (1909)

Georgie Fame (1943)
Mick Jones, *Clash* (1955)

Events: Sonny and Cher's divorce is finalized (1975).

June 27

Born: Helen Keller (1800)
Bob Keeshan [Captain Kangaroo] (1927)

Bruce Johnston (1944)

Events: Fillmore East closes (1971).

June 28

Born: Henry VII (1491)
Richard Rodgers (1902)
Lester Flatt (1914)

Dave Knight, *Procol Harum* (1945)
Gilda Radner

June 29

Born: Nelson Eddy (1901)   Little Eva (1945)
Fatty Arbuckle (1933)   Garland Jeffries

Died: Shorty Long [drowned] (1969)   Lowell George [stroke] (1979)
Tim Buckley [drug overdose]
(1975)

Events: *The Thin Man,* starring William Powell and Myrna Loy, opens (1934).

Jimi Hendrix gives his last show with *The Experience* in Denver.
Forty thousand fans storm the stage (1969).

June 30

Born: Buddy Rich (1917)   Glen Shorrock, *The Little River*
Dave Van Ronk (1936)   *Band* (1944)
Florence Ballard, *The Supremes*   Andrew Scott, *Sweet* (1949)
(1943)   Stanley Clarke (1951)

Events: The United States Congress does not extend the draft laws, ending
the draft (1971).

Gregg Allman and Cher wed (1975).

*John Cougar
Mellencamp*

Rick
Nelson

Billy
Joel

JULY

July 1

Born: Charles Laughton (1899)   Deborah Harry (1946)
Olivia deHavilland (1916)   Marc Benno (1947)
Delaney Bramlett (1939)   Dan Aykroyd (1949)

Events: Rin Tin Tin's first movie, *Where the North Begins,* is released (1923).

The Zip Code goes into use (1963).

Ralph Nader announces that rock music may cause impaired hearing (1969).

July 2

Born: Arthur Treacher (1894)   Joe Puerta, *Ambrosia* (1951)
Roy Bittan, *E Street Band* (1949)

Died: President James Garfield   Ernest Hemingway [suicide]
[assassination] (1881)   (1961)

Events: Jose Feliciano has his first New York City appearance at Gerde's Folk City (1963).

Lyndon B. Johnson signs the Civil Rights Bill (1964).

Leslie West and Felix Pappalardi form *Mountain* (1969).

July 3

Born: George M. Cohan (1878)   Paul Barrere, *Little Feat* (1948)
Mississippi John Hurt (1893)

Died: Brian Jones [drowns] (1969)   Jim Morrison [heart failure]
(1971)

Events: John Wayne wins his first Oscar, after 200 films, for playing Rooster Cogburn in *True Grit* (1969).

Brian Wilson performs live with *The Beach Boys* for the first time in twelve years. Seventy-four thousand attend in Anaheim Stadium (1976).

David Bowie retires for the first time in London (1973).

Journey's "Departure" LP goes gold (1980).

July 4

Born:

United States (1776)
Stephen Foster (1826)
Louis Armstrong (1900)
Gina Lollobrigida (1928)

Bill Withers (1938)
Jeremy Spencer, ex-*Fleetwood Mac* (1948)
John Waite (1955)

Events: Lewis Carroll first tells little Alice the story *Alice in Wonderland* (1862).

Fillmore West closes (1971).

July 5

Born: P.T. Barnum (1810)

Robbie Robertson, *The Band* (1943)

Events: *The Rolling Stones* hold their first United States recording session in Los Angeles (1965).

The Doors' "Light My Fire" breaks traditional AM radio format at six minutes, fifty seconds (1967).

July 8

Born:

John D. Rockefeller (1839)
Nelson Rockefeller (1908)
Billy Eckstine (1914)

Steve Lawrence (1935)
Jai Johanny Johansen, *The Allman Brothers Band* (1944)

Events: The Liberty Bell is cracked (1835).

The Everly Brothers start a 13-week summer-replacement TV show (1970).

July 9

Born:

Lee Hazelwood (1929)
O.J. Simpson (1947)

Bon Scott (1949)

Events: *Murder Man*, starring James Stewart in his first film, opens (1935).

The *Crosby, Stills, Nash & Young* reunion tour starts (1974).

July 10

Born: Arlo Guthrie (1947)

Dave Smally, *Raspberries* (1949)

Died: Jelly Roll Morton (1941)

Arthur Fiedler (1979)

Events: "Your Hit Parade" premieres on NBC-TV (1950).

Cher files for divorce from Gregg Allman (1975).

July 11

Born: John Quincy Adams (1767)   Terri Garthwaite, *Joy of*
              Blind Lemon Jefferson (1897)   *Cooking* (1938)
              Yul Brynner (1916)   Leon Spinks [ex-heavyweight
              Tab Hunter (1931)   champion] (1953)

Died: George Gershwin [during tumor operation] (1937)

Events: *Blind Faith* begins a tour of the United States (1969).

              "Bop 'Till You Drop" by Ry Cooder becomes the first digital rock LP
              (1979).

July 12

Born: Bill Cosby (1937)   Christine McVie, *Fleetwood*
              Connie Francis (1938)   *Mac* (1943)
                                          Walter Egan (1948)

Died: Minnie Ripperton [cancer] (1979)

Events: Screen Actors Guild holds its first meeting (1933).

              Janis Joplin premieres *The Full Tilt Boogie Band* (1970).

              Keith Harraway of Essex, England, establishes a world's record by
              blowing 169 smoke rings from one puff of a cigarette (1974).

July 13

Born: Julius Caesar (100 B.C.)   [Jim] Roger McGuinn (1942)
              Dave Garroway (1913)

Died: Billy the Kid (1881)

Events: *Queen* releases their first LP after eighteen months of rehearsal and
              recording (1973).

              The second Great New York City Blackout occurs (1977).

              Steve Dahl of WLUP Chicago stages the Disco Demolition and
              causes a riot in Comisky Park (1979).

              Live Aid Concert held concurrently in Philadelphia at JFK Stadium
              and in London at Wembley Arena, which included 40 bands, ran for
              16 hours and was seen by 1.6 billion people in 156 countries (1985).

July 14

Born: Woody Guthrie (1912)
Ingmar Bergman (1918)
John Chancellor (1927)

Jerry Rubin (1938)
Bob Scholl, *Mellow Kings* (1938)

Events: The New York World's Fair opens (1853).

Judy Collin's first New York appearance is at Gerde's Folk City (1964).

The Everly Brothers announce their official breakup (1973).

July 15

Born: Rembrandt (1606)
Linda Ronstadt (1946)
David Pack, *Ambrosia* (1952)

Larken Collins, *The Rossington-Collins Band* (1952)

Died: Julia Lennon [John's mother, in a car accident] (1952)

Events: George Gershwin has two funerals at the same time in New York City and Los Angeles. His body was in New York City (1937).

The Mariner Four transmits the first pictures of Mars (1965).

July 16

Born: Barbara Stanwyck (1907)
Ginger Rogers (1911)
Desmond Dekker (1941)

Stewart Copeland,
The Police (1952)

Died: Harry Chapin [car accident] (1981)

Events: *Cream* is formed by Eric Clapton, Jack Bruce, and Ginger Baker (1966).

July 17

Born: Haile Selassie (1891)
James Cagney (1899)
Phyllis Diller (1917)
Spencer Davis (1941)

Geezer Butler, *Black Sabbath*
(1949)
Phoebe Snow (1952)

Died: John Coltrane [cancer] (1957)

Billie Holiday [drug overdose]
(1959)

Events: At the cost of $17 million, Disneyland opens (1955).

Yellow Submarine premieres at London's Pavilion (1968).

July 18

Born:
Red Skelton (1913)
John Glenn (1921)
Screamin' Jay Hawkins (1929)
Dion (1939)
Brian Auger (1939)
Martha Reeves (1941)

Danny McCullock, *The Animals* (1945)
Tim Lynch, *The Flaming Groovies* (1946)
Wally Bryson, *The Raspberries* (1949)

July 19

Born:
George McGovern (1922)
Bernie Leadon, ex-*Eagles* (1945)
Brian May, *Queen* (1947)

Keith Godchaux, ex-*Grateful Dead* (1948)

Died: Clarence White, *The Byrds* (1973)

Events: David Bowie opens in the stage version of *The Elephant Man* in Denver (1980).

July 20

Born:
Sir Edmund Hillary (1919)
Natalie Wood (1938)
John Lodge, *The Moody Blues* (1945)

Carlos Santana (1947)
Kim Carnes (1945)

Events: "Do You Believe in Magic" charts, the first for *The Lovin' Spoonful* (1965).

Jane Asher announces her engagement on a TV show. Paul, on the other hand, was hearing about the engagement for the first time while watching Jane on the show (1968).

The first man walks on the moon (1969).

July 21

Born:
Ernest Hemingway (1899)
Marshall McLuhan (1911)
Isaac Stern (1920)

Cat Stevens [Steve Georgiou] (1948)

Events: Marlon Brando's first movie, *The Men*, opens (1950).

July 22

Born: Rose Kennedy (1890)
Amy Vanderbilt (1908)
Jason Robards (1922)
George Clinton, *Parliament-Funkadelic* (1940)
Don Henley, *The Eagles* (1946)

Richard Davies, *Supertramp* (1944)
Estelle Bennett, *The Ronettes* (1946)
Al DiMeola (1954)

Died: John Dillinger [Public Enemy No. 1] (1934)

Events: "The Bobby Darin Amusement Company," a variety show, premieres on CBS-TV (1972).

July 23

Born: Cleveland Dunkin, *Penguins* (1935)
Tony Joe White (1943)
Slash, Guns N' Roses (1965)

Dino Danelli, *The Rascals* (1945)
Andy McKay, *Roxy Music* (1946)
David Essex (1947)

Events: The Telstar communications satellite is launched (1962).

Led Zeppelin's John Bonham and manager Peter Grant beat up a security guard at Oakland Stadium for his being rude to a child (1977).

July 24

Born: Mike Mainieri (1938)

Steve Goodman (1948)

Died: Bobby Ramirez, *Edgar Winter's White Trash* [knifed in the streets] (1972)

Events: "Like A Rolling Stone" by Bob Dylan charts (1965).

July 25

Born: Walter Brennan (1894)

Jim McCarty, *The Yardbirds* (1943)

Events: Bob Dylan goes electric and is booed at The Newport Folk Festival (1965).

"Cheap Thrills" by Janis Joplin and *Big Brother and the Holding Company* is released (1968).

July 26

Born: Brenton Wood (1941)
Mick Jagger (1943)

Roger Taylor, *Queen* (1949)

Events: *The Clash* debut their LP in America two years after its release in the United Kingdom (1979).

July 27

Born: Leo Durocher (1906)
Homer, *Homer and Jethro*
(1920)
Nick Reynolds, *Kingston Trio*
(1933)

Kim Fowley (1942)
Bobbie Gentry (1944)
Peggy Fleming (1948)
David Muse, *Firefall* (1949)
Paul Cook, *Sex Pistols* (1956)

Events: George Harrison announces his concerts for Bangladesh (1971).

July 28

Born: Rudy Vallee (1901)
Jackie Kennedy Onassis (1929)
George Cummings, *Dr. Hook*
(1938)
Rick Wright, *Pink Floyd* (1945)

Jonathan Edwards (1946)
Steve Took, *T Rex* (1949)
Terry Fox (1958)
Rachel Sweet (1962)

Events: *Ned Kelly* starring Mick Jagger opens (1970).

Watkins Glen, with *The Grateful Dead, The Allman Brothers Band,* and *The Band,* draws 600,000 fans (1973).

July 29

Born: Dag Hammarskjold (1905)
Neil Doughty, *Reo Speedwagon*
(1946)

Geddy Lee, *Rush* (1950)

Died: Mama Cass Elliott [chokes; Keith Moon dies in the same London flat years later] (1974)

Events: *Help,* starring *The Beatles,* premieres (1965).

Bob Dylan nearly dies in a motorcycle accident (1966).

July 30

Born: Henry Ford (1863)
Casey Stengel (1891)
Buddy Guy (1936)
Ed "Kookie" Byrnes (1938)

Paul Anka (1941)
Jeffrey Hammond-Hammond,
Jethro Tull (1958)
Kate Bush (1958)

Events: *Small Talk,* the first Our Gang comedy, is released (1929).

Elvis makes his debut as a public performer (1954).

"Wild Thing," by *The Troggs,* charts (1966).

The Beatles close the Apple Boutique (1970).

The Rolling Stones fire Allen Klein as their manager (1970).

July 31

Born: Curt Gowdy (1919)   Bob Welch (1946)
              Ahmet Ertegun (1923)   Hugh MacDowell, *ELO* (1953)

Died: Franz Liszt (1886)   Jim Reeves (1964)

Events: The Concerts for Bangladesh, sponsored by George Harrison and featuring almost everybody onstage, are held in New York City (1971).

AUGUST

August 1

Born: Francis Scott Key (1779)
Herman Melville (1819)
Ramblin' Jack Elliott (1931)

Jerry Garcia (1942)
Dennis Paxton, *The Dave Clark Five,* (1943)

Died: Johnny Burnette [drowned] (1964)

Events: The first United States census is taken (1790).

Desert Fury, Burt Lancaster's first film, is released (1947).

Performance, starring Mick Jagger, is released (1968).

Music Television (MTV) begins broadcasting on cable TV (1981).

August 2

Born: Myrna Loy (1905)
Peter O'Toole (1933)
Edward Patten, *The Pips* (1939)

Garth Hudson, *The Band* (1937)
Andrew Gold (1951)

Died: Brian Cole, *The Association* [drug overdose] (1972)

Events: Johnny Cash signs with CBS Records (1958).

Max Romeo's "Wet Dream" charts in the United Kingdom, against official BBC ban of the song (1969).

August 3

Born: Beverly Lee, *The Shirelles* (1941)
John Klemmer (1946)
James Hetfield, Metallica (1963)

John Graham, *Electric Light Orchestra* (1951)

Died: Lenny Bruce [Leonard Alfred Schneider, drug overdose] (1966)

Events: Paul McCartney forms *Wings* (1971).

"Get The Knack" tops the LP chart and "My Sharona" tops the single charts for *The Knack* (1979).

August 4

Born: Elsberry Hobbs, *The Drifters*   Rick Derringer (1947)
              (1936)   Paul Leyton, *The Seekers* (1947)
              Frankie Ford (1940)

Events: Several United States radio stations ban *The Beatles* because John
              says they "are bigger than God" (1966).

              Jim Morrison passes out drunk on the porch of an old lady's house, and
              he's arrested one day before his Miami indecent exposure trial (1970).

August 5

Born: Neil Armstrong (1930)   Jimmy Webb (1946)
              Rick Huxley, *Dave Clark Five*   *Airto (1951)*
              (1942)
              Sammi Smith (1943)

Died: Marilyn Monroe [cause of   Pete Meadow [*Who* manager,
              Monroe's death disputable]   drug overdose] (1978)
              (1962)

Events: Dick Clark's "American Bandstand" begins in Philadelphia (1957).

              The Beatles release "Revolver" (1966).

              "The Piper At The Gates Of Dawn" becomes *Pink Floyd*'s first hit (1967).

August 6

Born: Lucille Ball (1911)   Mike Elliott (1929)
              Robert Mitchum (1917)   Isaac Hayes (1938)
              Andy Warhol (1927)

Events: Yippie Day at Disneyland — Yippies cause all sorts of problems for
              park officials (1970).

              Stevie Wonder nearly dies in a car crash in North Carolina (1973).

August 7

Born: Stan Freberg (1926)   Andy Frazier, *Free* (1952)
              Rahsaan Roland Kirk (1936)

Died: Homer, *Homer and Jethro* (1959)

Events: "The Twist" by Chubby Checker charts, becomes a national craze
              (1960).

              "It Ain't Me Babe," by *The Turtles,* charts (1965).

August 8

Born: Esther Williams (1923)   "Crissy Boy" Thompson,
        Joe Tex (1933)   *Madness* (1958)
        Dustin Hoffman (1937)   Dave "The Edge" Evans (1961)

Died: Cannonball Adderley (1975)

Events: *War Hunt*, Robert Redford's first film, opens (1962).

"House of the Rising Sun" becomes *The Animals'* first hit (1964).

Boston's debut LP is released by Epic and becomes the fastest-selling premiere in record history, after every other major label rejected the demos (1976).

August 9

Born: Barbara Mason (1947)

Died: Sharon Tate and friends   Lillian Roxon [Rock
        [the Manson murders] (1969)   Encyclopedia, asthma] (1973)

Events: Robert Zimmerman legally changes his name to Bob Dylan (1962).

"Ready, Steady, Go" premieres on British TV (1963).

August 10

Born: Jimmy Dean [Seth Ward] (1928)   Ronnie Spector (1947)
        Eddie Fisher (1928)   Ian Anderson, *Jethro Tull* (1947)
        Bobby Hatfield, *The Righteous*   Eric Braum, *Iron Butterfly*
        Brothers (1940)   (1950)

Events: "Summertime Blues" by Eddie Cochran charts (1958).

"Chantilly Lace" by The Big Bopper charts (1958).

"Layla" by *Derek* [Eric Clapton] *and the Dominoes* charts (1972).

Paul and Linda McCartney are arrested for drugs in Sweden (1972).

The Son of Sam is captured after a search of one year, twelve days in New York City (1977).

August 11

Born: Mike Douglas (1925)   Jeff Hanna, *The Dirt Band* (1947)
Dennis Payton, *The Dave Clark*   Eric Carmen (1949)
Five (1943)   Joe Jackson

Events: The first sound on film process is patented (1906).

The Rolling Stones play a jazz festival headlined by Acker Bilk (1963).

August 12

Born: Cecil B. DeMille (1881)   Sam Andrew, *Big Brother and*
Wilt [Big Dipper] Chamberlain   *the Holding Company* (1941)
(1936)   Mark Knopfler, *Dire Straits*
Buck [Alvin] Owens (1939)   (1949)

Events: Fleetwood Mac makes their first appearance at the National Jazz and Blues Festival in England (1967).

Janis Joplin gives her final concert, Harvard (1970).

The first space shuttle is tested (1977).

"Badlands" by Bruce Springsteen hits the charts (1978).

August 13

Born: Annie Oakley (1860)   Tony Santini, *Sha Na Na* (1948)
Alfred Hitchcock (1899)   Dan Fogelberg (1951)
Fidel Castro (1927)

Died: King Curtis [knifed] (1971)

Events: The One-to-One Concerts to benefit retarded kids are held, headlined by John and Yoko, Stevie Wonder, and *Sha Na Na,* among others, in Madison Square Garden (1972).

August 14

Born: Buddy Greco (1926)   Tim Bogert (1944)
Dash Crofts (1938)   Susan St. James (1946)
David Crosby (1941)

Died: Big Bill Broonzy [cancer] (1958)   Gladys Presley [Elvis' mom]
(1958)

Events: VJ Day: Japan surrenders to MacArthur ending World War II in the Pacific (1945).

"Hang On Sloopy," *The McCoys*' [Rick Derringer] first hit, charts (1965)

The Family Dog, San Francisco's top hippie venue, closes (1970).

August 15

Born:

Sir Walter Scott (1771)
Napoleon (1769)
Lawrence of Arabia (1888)
Julia Child (1912)
Bobby Helms (1933)

Peter York, *Spencer Davis Group* (1942)
Tommy Aldridge, *Black Oak Arkansas* (1950)

Events:

Thomas Edison makes the first recording: "Mary had a little lamb" (1877).

Panama Canal opens (1914).

Elvis and Colonel Parker sign a management deal. Their handshake agreement is a myth (1955).

Woodstock Music and Arts Fair opens on Max Yasgur's farm for three days of peace and music (1969).

"Slow Train Coming," Bob Dylan's testament to Christianity, is released (1979).

August 16

Born:

George Meany (1894)
Fess Parker [Davy Crockett] (1927)
Robert Culp (1930)
Eydie Gorme (1931)
Chris Curtis, *The Searchers* (1941)

Kevin Ayers (1945)
Gary Loizzo, *American Breed* (1945)
Madonna (1959)

Died:

Elvis Presley (1977)

Events:

Robert Fulton invents the steamboat (1807).

Pete Best is fired from *The Beatles* and replaced by Ringo Starr (1962).

The Ramones premiere at CBGB (and OMFUG) in New York City (1974).

Robert Plant almost kills himself and his wife in a car wreck in Greece (1975).

August 17

Born: Sib Hashian, *Boston* (1949)   Belinda Carlisle (1958)

Died: Paul Williams, *The Temptations* [suicide] (1973)

Events: Joan Baez introduces Bob Dylan to 14,000 at Forest Hills. He sings three songs with her and escapes the New York City folk scene forever (1963).

Woodstock closes, and the generation returns to everyday realities (1969).

John Phillips, *The Mamas and the Papas,* is charged with operating a cocaine ring (1980).

August 18

Born: Robert Redford (1937)   Dennis Elliott, ex-*Foreigner*
Carl Wayne, *The Move* (1944)   (1950)
Nona Hendryx (1945)

Events: Mick Jagger is accidentally shot on the set of *Ned Kelly* (1969).

Nick Lowe and Carlene Carter wed (1979).

August 19

Born: Orville Wright [Wright Brothers,   Ian Gillan (1945)
    airplane inventors] (1871)   John Deacon, *Queen* (1951)
Ginger Baker (1939)   Jason Starkey [Ringo's son]
Johnny Nash (1940)   (1967)
Billy J. Kramer (1943)

Died: Groucho Marx (1977)

Events: The second United States tour by *The Beatles* starts in The Cow Palace, San Francisco (1964).

"Who Are You," the last LP featuring Keith Moon, is released (1978).

August 20

Born: Jim Reeves (1924)   Robert Anthony Plant,
Jacqueline Susann (1926)   *Led Zeppelin* (1948)
Jim Pankow, *Chicago* (1947)   Phil Lynott, *Thin Lizzie* (1951)

Died: George Jackson (1971)

Events: "Rock Around The Clock" reaches No. 1 for *Bill Haley and the Comets* (1955).

John and Yoko begin recording "Double Fantasy," his last LP (1980).

August 21

Born: Count Basie (1904)   Jackie DeShannon (1944)
         Kenny Rogers (1938)   Joe Strummer, *The Clash* (1952)

Events: The first French-European Punk Rock Festival is held without *The Sex Pistols,* who were too much for the promoters (1976).

Linda Ronstadt opens on Broadway as Mabel in *Pirates of Penzance* (1980).

August 22

Born: John Lee Hooker (1917)   Fred Milano, *The Belmonts* (1939)
         Bob Flannigan, *The Four   Donna Godchaux, ex-*Grateful
           Freshmen* (1926)   Dead* (1947)
         Dale Hawkins [wrote "Suzy Q"]   Ian Mitchell, *Bay City Rollers*
           (1938)   (1958)

Events: Handel begins work on "Messiah" (1741).

BBC-TV begins regular transmissions (1936).

Elvis makes his live comeback, starring four nights at Las Vegas' International Hotel. These are his first live shows since 1961 and perhaps the all-time greatest comeback in entertainment history (1969).

"Foreigner 4" is released (1982).

August 23

Born: Gene Kelly (1912)   Keith Moon (1947)
         Rudy Lewis, *The Drifters* (1936)

Events: John Lennon and Cynthia Powell wed (1962).

"She Loves You" is released by *The Beatles* (1963).

Help, The Beatles' second movie, is released (1965).

Lou Reed and *The Velvet Underground* play their last gig together. He didn't let the band know in advance or even later; he just quit (1970).

August 24

Born:
Cardinal Cushing (1895)
William Winfeld, *The Harptones* (1929)
David Frielberg, *Jefferson Starship* (1938)
Ernie Wright, *The Imperials* (1939)
John Cipollina, *Quicksilver Messenger Service* (1943)
Jim Capaldi, *Traffic* (1944)
Ken Hensley, *Uriah Heep* (1945)
Dave Hlubek, *Molly Hatchet* (1951)

Events:
Mt. Vesuvius erupts (A.D. 79).

Dolly Madison saves George Washington's portrait from the White House as the British set it afire (1814).

Captain Webb is the first to swim the English Channel (1875).

The Rolling Stones meet Allen Klein for the first time (1965).

"In-A-Gadda-Da-Vida," by *Iron Butterfly,* charts (1968).

Billboard gives NWEW-FM the "Greatest Radio Station in the World" award (1975).

Mark Chapman, John Lennon's assassin, gets 20-years-to-life in prison (1982).

Vince Van Patten and *Loverboy* singer Mike Reno are victorious at the First Music and Tennis Festival in Atlanta, Georgia (1982).

August 25

Born:
Ivan the Terrible (1530)
Ruby Keeler (1910)
Leonard Bernstein (1918)
George Wallace (1919)
Sean Connery (1930)
Wayne Shorter, *Weather Report* (1933)
Gene Simmons, *Kiss* (1949)
Elvis Costello (1954)

Died: Stan Kenton (1979)

Events:
"Sherry," *The Four Seasons'* first hit, is released (1962).

"Cars" by Gary Numan is released (1979).

August 26

Born: Willie Rush, *Asbury Jukes* (1952)

Died: Lee Hays [heart attack] (1981)

Events:
Women win the right to vote (1920).

The third Isle of Wight Pop Festival is held (1970).

"Ca Plan Pour Moi" by *Plastic Bertrand* is released (1978).

August 27

Born: Sam Goldwyn [MGM] (1882)
Lyndon B. Johnson (1908)
Lester Young [jazz sax player] (1909)
Martha Raye (1916)
Phil Shulmon, *Gentle Giant* (1937)

Simon Kirke, *Bad Company* (1949)
Willie "Mink" DeVille (1950)
Glen Matlock, *The Sex Pistols* (1956)
Alex Lifeson, *Rush* (1953)

Died: Brian Epstein, [*The Beatles*" first manager; drug overdose] (1967)

Events: "Highway 61 Revisited," Bob Dylan's first rock LP, is released (1965).

August 28

Born: Leo Tolstoy (1828)
Charles Boyer (1899)
Dan Serephine, *Chicago* (1948)

Mary McCartney [Paul and Lindas daughter] (1969)

Events: Martin Luther King delivers the "I have a dream" speech (1963).

Bob Dylan introduces *The Beatles* to smoking pot in the Delmonico Hotel, New York (1964).

The Rolling Stones announce a management deal with Allen Klein (1965).

August 29

Born: Ingrid Bergman (1915)
Charlie "Bird" Parker (1920)
Dinah Washington (1924)

Elliot Gould (1938)
Michael Jackson (1958)

Events: George Harrison joins *The Quarrymen,* a band already including John Lennon and Paul McCartney (1958).

"Oh Pretty Woman," by Roy Orbison, charts (1964).

The Beatles play their final concert together in Candlestick Park, San Francisco, although nobody knew it at the time. They did perform for free atop Apple's London building in 1969 in public, however (1966).

The final episode of "The Fugitive" starring David Janssen airs. He catches the one-armed man, gets him to confess, but loses him to death; but, the police hear it all (1967).

August 30

Born: Huey Long (1893)   Jean-Claude Killy (1943)
              Fred MacMurray (1908)   Chuck Colbert, *American*
              Shirley Booth (1909)   *Breed* (1944)
              John Phillips, *The Mamas and*
                the Papas (1935)

Events: The United States to Russia hotline is installed (1963).

              The Beatles release their first Apple record, "Hey Jude/Revolution"
              (1968).

August 31

Born: Fredric March (1897)   Jerry Allison, *The Crickets*
              Ted Williams (1918)   (1939)
              James Coburn (1927)   Van Morrison (1945)
              Eldridge Cleaver (1935)   Rick Roberts, *Firefall* (1949)

Events: Lyndon B. Johnson signs the Food Stamp Bill (1964).

              Bob Dylan makes £38,000 for a one-hour show at the second Isle of
              Wight Festival (1969).

              Led Zeppelin's "In Through The Out Door" enters *Billboard* at No. 1.
              No single is released. The LP has nine different covers, wrapped in
              brown paper to conceal which is being bought (1979).

              Pope John Paul II's LP is released (1979).

SEPTEMBER

September 1

Born: Tommy Evans, *The Drifters* (1927)   Archie Bell (1944)
Conway Twitty [Harold Lloyd   Barry Gibb (1946)
Jenkins] (1933)

Events: Sonny and Cher premiere on CBS-TV with their variety show (1971).

Clayton Moore, TV's Lone Ranger, loses a civil suit over his right to the black mask he wore. The company with the copyright releases a movie with a younger actor that flops (1979).

September 2

Born: Cleveland Amory (1917)   Rosalind Ashford,
Horace Silver (1928)   *The Vandellas,* (1943)
Joe Simon (1943)

Died: J.R.R. Tolkien, author of *Lord of the Rings* (1973).

Events: *The Hunchback of Notre Dame,* starring Lon Chaney, opens (1923).

George Harrison and Olivia Arias wed (1978).

The *Animal House* soundtrack is released (1978).

September 3

Born: Memphis Slim [Peter Chatman]   George Biondo, *Steppenwolf*
(1916)   (1945)
Al Jardine, *The Beach Boys* (1942)   Don Brewer, *Grand Funk*
Mike Harrison (1945)   *Railroad* (1948)

Died: Woody Guthrie [Huntington's   Al "Blind Owl" Wilson (1970)
Disease] (1967)

Events: "96 Tears" by *? & The Mysterians* charts (1966).

September 4

Born: Richard Wright (1908)
Merald Knight, *Pips* (1942)
Gene Parsons, *The Byrds* (1945)
David Liebman (1946)
Gary Duncan, *Quicksilver Messenger Service* (1946)
Greg Elmore, *Quicksilver Messenger Service* (1946)
Martin Chambers, *The Pretenders* (1951)

September 5

Born: Jesse James (1847)
Raquel Welch (1940)
Loudon Wainwright III (1946)
Freddie Mercury [Fredrick Bulsara], *Queen* (1946)
Buddy Miles (1946)
"Clem" Clempson, *Humble Pie* (1949)

Events: "Do Wah Diddy," Manfred Mann's first hit, charts (1964).

September 6

Born: Lafayette (1757)
Joseph P. Kennedy (1888)
Roger Waters, *Pink Floyd* (1947)
Banner Thomas, *Molly Hatchet* (1954)

Events: George Harrison forms Dark Horse Records (1974).

September 7

Born: Grandma Moses (1860)
Peter Lawford (1923)
Little Milton (1934)
Buddy [Charles Hardin] Holly (1936)
Richard Rountree (1942)
Chrissie Hynde, *The Pretenders* (1951)

Died: Keith Moon, in the same London flat as Mama Cass years before (1978)

Events: "Suzy Q," *Creedence Clearwater Revival*'s first hit, charts (1968).

September 8

Born:

Jimmy C. Rogers (1897)
Sid Caesar (1922)
Peter Sellers (1925)
Patsy Cline (1932)
Ron "Pigpen" McKernan,
 Grateful Dead (1945)

Jose Feliciano (1945)
Will Lee (1950)
Zeke Snodgress Young [Neil
 and Carrie's son] (1972)

Events: "Star Trek" is seen on TV for the first time (1966).

Full, free, and absolute pardon is given to Richard Nixon by Gerald Ford for all offenses against the United States which he has committed or may have committed or taken part in (1974).

September 9

Born:

Colonel Sanders (1890)
Cliff Robertson (1925)
Jimmy Reed (1925)
Elvin Jones (1927)
Otis Redding (1941)

Luther Simmons, *The Main
 Ingredient* (1942)
Doug Ingle, *Iron Butterfly* (1945)
Billy Preston (1946)

Died: Mao Tse-tung (1976)

Events: Cat Stevens and Fouzia Ali wed (1979).

September 10

Born:

Arnold Palmer (1929)
Artie Tripp, *Mothers of
 Invention* (1939)
Roy Ayers (1940)
Danny Hutton, *Three Dog
 Night* (1942)

Barriemore Barlow, *Jethro Tull*
 (1949)
Don Powell, *Slade* (1950)
Joe Perry, *Aerosmith* (1950)
Johnny Fingers, *Boomtown
 Rats* (1956)

Events: "Last Train To Clarksville," *The Monkees'* first hit, charts (1966).

Cheap Trick replaces Tom Petersson with Pete Comita on bass (1980).

September 11

Born:

O. Henry (1862)
Hedy Lamarr (1915)

Phil May, *Pretty Things* (1944)

Died: Peter Tosh [murdered] (1987)

Events: Dylan's first New York City appearance at Gerde's Folk City (1961).

"The Great White Wonder," the most famous bootleg of all, featuring Bob Dylan, emerges (1969).

The *Jackson Five's* animated cartoon series debuts on ABC-TV (1971).

87

September 12

Born: Maurice Chevalier (1888)
Jesse Owens (1913)
Frank McGee (1921)
George Jones (1931)

Maria Muldaur (1943)
Gary Beckley, *America* (1952)
Nina Blackwood, MTV Video
Jock

Events: *The Monkees'* TV show premieres on NBC. It ran until 1968, then ran until 1972 on CBS, and until 1973 on ABC (1966).

The Woody Guthrie Memorial Concert at the Hollywood Bowl features Bob Dylan, Joan Baez, Arlo Guthrie, and others (1970).

The fourth (and final) Secret Policeman's Ball to aid Amnesty International is held with a stellar lineup in London (1981).

September 13

Born: Claudette Colbert (1907)
Bill Monroe (1911)
Mel Torme (1925)
David Clayton-Thomas, *Blood, Sweat and Tears* (1941)

Peter Cetera (1944)
Zak Starkey [Ringo's son] (1965)

Events: FCC amendment on payola becomes law and changes record promotion tactics (1960).

The Plastic Ono Band plays the Toronto Peace Festival featuring John, Yoko, and Eric Clapton (1970).

September 14

Born: Dante (1321)
"Bowser" Bauman, *Sha Na Na* (1947)

Paul Kossoff, *Free* (1950)

Died: Walter "Furry" Lewis [heart attack] (1981).

Events: "The Archie Show," featuring the cartoon characters, premieres on CBS-TV (1968).

Pink Floyd's The Wall movie starts production, and stars *The Boomtown Rats'* Bob Geldof (1981).

September 15

Born: Agatha Christie (1890)   Julian "Cannonball Adderley
             Jean Renoir (1894)   (1926)
             Roy Acuff (1903)   Lee Dorman, *Iron Butterfly*
             Jackie Cooper (1922)   (1942)
             Bobby Short (1926)

Died: Bill Evans [bleeding ulcers] (1980)

Events: Bill Cosby and Robert Culp star in the premiere of "I Spy" (1965).

             Abba's first United States tour starts (1980).

September 16

Born: J.C. Penney (1875)   Betty Kelly, *The Vandellas* (1944)
             Lauren Bacall (1924)   Kenny Jones, *The Who* (1948)
             B.B. King (1925)   Earl Klugh (1953)

Events: Play-Doh is introduced (1955).

             "Parallel Lines" by *Blondie* charts (1978).

             The Grateful Dead give a concert beside Egypt's great pyramids (1978).

September 17

Born: Hank Williams (1923)   Anne Bancroft (1931)
             Bill Black (1926)   Fee Waybill, *The Tubes* (1950)
             Roddy McDowell (1931)

Died: Marc Bolan, *T Rex* [car crash] (1977)

Events: The United States Constitution is signed (1787).

             RCA demonstrates the first 33-1/3 LPs and players. CBS has to completely rework the process to make it functional (1931).

             "M*A*S*H" premieres on CBS-TV (1972).

September 18

Born: Greta Garbo (1905)   Dee Dee Ramone [Doug Colvin]
            Frankie Avalon (1939)   (1961)

Died: Dag Hammarskjold (1961)   Jimi Hendrix [drug overdose]
                                                 (1970)

Events: The United States Capitol cornerstone is placed (1793).

Don Adams and Barbara Feldon star in the "Get Smart" TV premiere (1965).

Patty Hearst is arrested in San Francisco after more than a year on the FBI Most Wanted List (1975).

"Gross malpractice in the indiscriminate prescribing of prescription drugs" is charged against Dr. George Nichopolous, who gave Elvis ninety-five prescriptions from January to August 1977 (1979).

September 19

Born: Brook Benton (1931)   Mama Cass Elliot (1943)
            Brian Epstein (1934)   David Bromberg (1945)
            Mick Massi, *The Four Seasons*   Twiggy (1949)
            (1935)   Nile Rodgers (1952)
            Bill Medley, *The Righteous
            Brothers* (1940)

Died: Graham Parsons [drug overdose] (1973)

Events: General George Washington makes his farewell speech to the troops (1796).

LSD is proclaimed the sacrament of Timothy Leary's religion (1966).

MUSE concerts begin in New York City (1979).

Simon and Garfunkel reunite for intimate Central Park concert of 500,000. HBO movie and soundtrack follow (1981).

September 20

Born: Upton Sinclair (1878)   Sophia Loren (1934)

Died: Jim Croce [and five others, in a plane crash] (1973)

Events: George Harrison makes his first trip to India (1966).

Jim Morrison is found not guilty of lewd behavior. But he is found guilty of the indecent exposure rap; he appealed the decision (1970).

Paul McCartney is busted for growing pot on his farm in Scotland (1972).

September 21

Born: H.G. Wells (1866)
Don Preston, *Mothers of Invention* (1932)
Leonard Cohen (1934)

Donald Felder, *The Eagles* (1947)
Betty Wright (1953)

Events: "Wake Up Little Suzy" by *The Everly Brothers* charts (1957).

"All Along The Watchtower" by Jimi Hendrix charts (1968).

September 22

Born: George Chambers, *Chambers Brothers* (1931)
David Coverdale, *Deep Purple* (1949)

Joan Jett (1958)

Events: The ice cream cone is patented (1903).

"The Man From U.N.C.L.E." first appears on NBC-TV (1964).

September 23

Born: Augustus Caesar (63 B.C.)
Mickey Rooney (1920)
John Coltrane (1926)
Ray Charles (1932)

Roy Buchanan (1939)
Tim Rose (1940)
Bruce Springsteen (1949)

Died: Robbie McIntosh, *The Average White Band* [drug overdose] (1974)

Events: The "Paul McCartney is dead" rumor begins with an article in *Northern Star*, the newspaper of Illinois University (1969).

September 24

Born: F. Scott Fitzgerald (1896)
Anthony Newley (1931)
Gerry Marsden, *Gerry and the Pacemakers* (1942)

Linda Eastman McCartney (1942)
Jerry Donahue, *Fairport Convention* (1946)

Events: The Warren Commission announces that Lee Harvey Oswald "acted alone" in his alleged assassination of John F. Kennedy (1964).

September 25

Born: William Faulkner (1897)   John Locke, *Spirit* (1943)
             Barbara Walters (1931)   Burleigh Drummond, *Ambrosia*
             Joe Russell, *The Persuasions*   (1951)
             (1939)

Died: John Bonham, *Led Zeppelin* [alcohol overdose] (1980)

Events: Balboa discovers the Pacific (1513).

             Elvis performs his only show at the Grand Ole Opry (1954).

             Ed Sullivan begins his show in Sunday night (1955).

             Sonny Liston knocks out Floyd Patterson in the first round for the
             heavyweight title (1962).

             The Beatles' animated TV show debuts on ABC (1965).

September 26

Born: Johnny Appleseed (1774)   Joe Bauer, *The Youngbloods*
             T.S. Eliot (1888)   (1941)
             George Gershwin (1889)   Brian Ferry, *Roxy Music* (1946)
             Marty Robbins (1925)   Olivia Newton-John (1947)
             Dick Heckstall-Smith, *Alexis*
                Korner Band (1934)

Died: Bessie Smith (1937)

Events: The first gramophone patent is given to Emile Berliner (1887).

             Eddie Fisher and Debbie Reynolds wed (1955).

             The first of four Kennedy-Nixon debates is held (1960).

             The first episode of "The Beverly Hillbillies" airs on CBS-TV (1962).

             "You Really Got Me," *The Kinks'* first hit, charts (1964).

             Billy Joel's "52nd Street" tour opens in New Haven (1978).

             "The Long Run" is released, the last *Eagles* studio LP (1979).

September 27

Born: Samuel Adams (1722)   Meat Loaf [Marvin Aday] (1947)
             Senator Sam Ervin (1896)   Robbie "Basspeare"
             Don Nix (1942)   Shakespeare (1953)
             Randy Bachman (1943)
Died: *Cliff Burton, Metallica [bus crash] (1986)*
Events: "Blueberry Hill" by Fats Domino charts (1956).

             Bob Dylan gets his first *New York Times* review (1962).

September 28

Born: Ed Sullivan (1902)   Nick St. Nicholas, *Steppenwolf*
Al Capp (1909)   (1943)
Brigitte Bardot (1934)   Helen Shapiro (1946)
Ben E. King [Nelson] (1938)

Died: Jimmy McCulloch, *Wings* (1979)

Events: Bing Crosby and David Bowie record a duet of "Peace On Earth,"
but Crosby dies before it can be seen or released (1977).

September 29

Born: Gene Autry (1907)   Mike Pinera, *IronButterfly*
Jerry Lee Lewis (1935)   (1948)
Jean-Luc Ponty (1942)   Suzzy Roche, *The Roches*
Mark Farner, *Grand Funk*   (1956)
Railroad (1948)

Events: Bob Dylan has his first recording session, playing guitar and mouth
harp behind Carolyn Hester's first CBS record. Producer John Hammond later signs Dylan (1961).

The Rolling Stones start their first United Kingdom tour with *The
Everly Brothers* (1963).

September 30

Born: Lester Maddox (1915)   Dewey Martin, *Poco* (1942)
Deborah Kerr (1921)   Gus Dudgeon (1942)
Truman Capote (1924)   Frankie Lymon (1942)
Angie Dickinson (1932)   Sylvia Peterson, *The Chiffons*
Johnny Mathis (1935)   (1946)
Freddy King (1935)   Patrice Rushen (1954)

Died: James Dean [car crash] (1955)

Events: The Hoover Dam is dedicated (1935).

"The Flintstones" debuts on TV (1960).

Cesar Chavez founds the Farmworkers Union (1962).

The "Uncle Floyd Show" premieres in New Jersey on WBTB-TV (1975).

"Louie, Louie" by John Belushi from *Animal House* is released (1978).

"Are We Not Men," *Devo*'s first hit, is released (1978).

Jan Hammer

Flo and Eddie

OCTOBER

October 1

Born:
Walter Matthau (1920)
George Peppard (1928)
Richard Harris (1933)
Julie Andrews (1935)
Scott McKenzie (1944)

Herbert Rhodes, *The*
Persuasions (1944)
Donny Hathaway (1945)
"Cub" Koda, *Brownsville*
Station (1949)

Events:
Pink Floyd arrives in the United States for their first tour (1967).

Elton John opens his first of eight sold-out nights in Madison Square Garden (1979)

The Beatles catalogue is released on half-speed by Mobile Fidelity at $325 a set in limited quantity (1982).

Queen's "The Game" goes platinum (1980).

October 2

Born:
Mahatma Gandhi (1869)
Groucho Marx (1898)
Rex Reed (1939)
Don McLean (1945)
Michael Rutherford, *Genesis*
(1950)

Sting (Gordon Sumner), *The*
Police (1951)
Phil Oakley, *The Human*
League (1955)

Events:
The Grateful Dead are busted in their communal home at 710 Ashbury Street, San Francisco. The bust is meaningless, because there is no warrant (1967).

October 3

Born:
Gore Vidal (1925)
James Darren (1936)
Eddie Cochran (1938)

Chubby Checker (1941)
Lindsey Buckingham (1947)
Ronnie Laws (1950)

Events:
"The Adventures of Ozzie and Harriet" premieres on ABC-TV (1952).

Bruce Springsteen and the E Street Band open their "River" tour in Ann Arbor, Michigan, with a total of 139 dates of 3-1/2 to 4 hours each show (1980).

October 4

Born: Frederic Remington [artist] (1861)
Damon Runyon (1884)
Buster Keaton (1895)

Charlton Heston (1923)
Roger Moore (1927)
James Fielder, *Blood, Sweat and Tears* (1947)

Died: Janis Joplin [drug overdose] (1970)

Events: "Ted Mack's Amateur Hour" premieres on NBC-TV (1949).

USSR launches *Sputnik*, the first satellite (1957).

October 5

Born: Chester Arthur (1830)
Bill [Jose Jiminez] Dana (1924)
Carlo Mastrangelo, *The Belmonts* (1938)

Steve Miller (1943)
Brian Connolly, *Sweet* (1948)

Events: "Tom Dooley" charts, *The Kingston Trio*'s first hit (1958).

The Beatles release "Love Me Do" (1962).

"White Room" is released by *Cream* (1968).

Oregon becomes the first state to decriminalize pot (1973).

Poet Dylan Thomas [Bob Dylan used his name] is buried in Poet's Corner, Westminster Abbey, England (1981).

October 6

Born: Carole Lombard (1908)   Thor Heyerdahl (1914)

Died: Anwar El-Sadat [assassinated] (1981)

Events: LSD is declared illegal in the United States (1966).

Hippies perform a Hippie funeral in San Francisco (1967).

Cat Olsen robs a bank in Greenwich Village, calls Scott Muni at WNEW-FM, and asks him to play some *Grateful Dead* (1975).

October 7

Born: June Allyson (1923)   Tony Sylvester, *Main*
              Al Martino (1927)   *Ingredient* (1941)
              Dino Valenti (1940)   Gary Puckett (1942)

Died: Edgar Allen Poe (1849)   Johnny Kidd [car crash] (1966)

Events: Dick Clark's first network broadcast of "American Bandstand" is on
              ABC-TV (1957).

              Janis Joplin is cremated in Los Angeles (1970).

October 8

Born: Eddie Rickenbacker (1890)   Johnny Ramone (1948)
              Doc Green, *The Drifters* (1934)   Michael Rose, *The Average*
              Reverend Jesse Jackson (1941)   *White Band* (1949)

Events: The Chicago Fire occurs (1871).

              The Sex Pistols are signed by EMI (1976).

              "The Stranger" LP by Billy Joel is released (1977).

October 9

Born: E. Howard Hunt (1918)   John Entwistle (1946)
              Pat Burke, *The Foundations*   Jackson Browne (1949)
                (1937)   Sean Ono Lennon [John and
              John Winston Lennon (1940)   Yoko's son] (1975)

Events: Judge Irving Kaufman rules that John Lennon's pot conviction in
              Britain is not cause for deportation (1976).

October 10

Born: Helen Hayes (1900)   Keith Reid, *Procol Harum*
              Thelonious Monk (1918)   (1946)
              Harold Pinter (1930)   John Prine (1946)
              Alan Cartwright, *Procol Harum*   David Lee Roth, *Van Halen*
                (1945)   (1955)

Events: Frank Zappa's first solo LP, "Hot Rats," is released (1969).

              Spiro T. Agnew resigns as vice president of the United States (1973).

October 11

Born: Eleanor Roosevelt (1884)
Daryl Hall, *Hall and Oates* (1946)
Gary Mallaber, *Steve Miller Band* (1946)

Greg Douglas, *Steve Miller Band* (1949)
Mark Goodman, MTV Video Jock

Events: *To Have And Have Not* starring Humphrey Bogart and Lauren Bacall opens (1944).

Muddy Waters is almost killed in a car wreck (1969).

October 12

Born: Dick Gregory (1932)
Sam Moore, *Sam and Dave* (1935)

Rick Parfitt, *Status Quo* (1948)

Died: Gene Vincent [bleeding ulcers] (1971)

Events: Nikita Krushchev pounds his shoe on a table at the United Nations (1960).

October 13

Born: Lenny Bruce (1925)
Margaret Hilda Roberts Thatcher (1925)
Paul Simon (1942)

Robert Lamm, *Chicago* (1944)
Sammy Hagar (1947)
Craig McGregor, *Foghat* (1949)

Events: The Pittsburgh Pirates beat the New York Yankees for their first World Series Championship since 1925 (1960).

October 14

Born: William Penn (1644)
Dwight D. "Ike" Eisenhower (1890)
Bill Justis (1926)

Cliff Richard [Harry Rogers Webb] (1940)
Justin Hayward, *The Moody Blues* (1946)

Died: Errol Flynn (1959)

Bing Crosby (1977)

Events: Alvin and the Chipmunks have their first TV show (1961).

Each member of *Kiss* releases a separate solo effort (1978).

AC/DC's "Let There Be Rock" and "If You Want Blood" go gold (1980).

October 15

Born: Mario Puzo (1921)   Richard Carpenter (1945)
Barry McGuire (1935)   Tito Jackson (1953)

Events: Charlie Chaplin's first talkie, *The Great Dictator,* opens (1940).

Derek and the Dominoes kick off their United States tour (1970).

"Tusk" by *Fleetwood Mac* is released at the cost of $1 million (1979).

October 16

Born: Oscar Wilde (1854)   CF Turner, *Bachman-Turner*
Eugene O'Neill (1888)   *Overdrive* (1943)
Bert Kaempfert (1923)   Bob "Ace" Weir, *The*
Charles Colson (1931)   *Grateful Dead* 91947)

Died: Leonard Chess [Chess Records founder, heart attack] (1969)

Events: The New York Mets win the World Series (1969).

October 17

Born: Arthur Miller (1915)   Evel Knievel (1938)
Rita Hayworth (1918)   Jimmy Seals, *Seals and Crofts*
Montgomery Clift (1920)   (1942)
Jimmy Breslin (1930)

Events: Thomas Edison files a patent for the optical phonograph — the first movie (1888).

October 18

Born: Chuck Berry (1926)   Laura Nyro (1947)
George C. Scott (1927)   Gary Richrath, *REO*
Ronnie Bright, *The Coasters*   *Speedwagon* (1949)
(1938)

Events: The Grand Ole Opry opens (1925).

"How I Won The War," John Lennon's first non-Beatle movie, opens (1967).

Led Zeppelin has their first gig in London with their new name (1968).

Richard Nader's first rock 'n' roll revival at Madison Square Garden (1969).

"Come Together," the first single from the last LP by *The Beatles,* charts (1969).

October 19

Born:

John Adams (1735)
Jack Anderson (1922)
David Guard, *The Kingston Trio*
  (1934)

Peter Tosh (1944)
Jeannie C. Riley (1945)

Events:

The Yardbirds, with Jimmy Page and Jeff Beck on guitars, start their United States tour (1966).

The Specials release their debut LP with Elvis Costello as producer (1979).

October 20

Born:

Art Buchwald (1925)
Dr. Joyce Brothers (1928)
Mickey Mantle (1931)

Ric Lee, *Ten Years After* (1945)
Al Greenwood, *Foreigner* (1951)
Tom Petty (1953)

Died:

Ronnie Van Zant and Steve Gaines, from *Lynyrd Skynyrd,* in a plane crash (1977).

Events:

At The Circus by the Marx Brothers opens (1939).

Jesus Christ Superstar opens on Broadway (1971).

October 21

Born:

Alfred Nobel (1833)
Dizzy Gillespie (1917)
Norman Wright, *Del-Vikings*
  (1937)
Steve Cropper (1941)
Manfred Mann (1941)
Elvin Bishop (1942)
Lee Loughnane, *Chicago* (1946)

Charlotte Caffey, *The Go-Go's*
  (1953)
Eric Faulkner, *Bay City Rollers*
  (1955)
Jade Jagger [Mick and Bianca's
  daughter] (1971)
Astrella Celeste Leitch
  [Donovan's daughter] (1971)

Died:

Jack Kerouac [started "Beat Generation"] (1969)

Events:

Buddy Holly does his final recording session (1958).

October 22

Born:

Franz Liszt (1811)
Sarah Bernhardt (1844)
Timothy Leary (1920)

Annette Funicello (1952)
Leslie West (1945)
Eddie Brigato, *The Rascals* (1946)

Events:

EMI Records passes on the signing of *The High Numbers,* the group that became *The Who* (1964).

"Good Vibrations" charts for *The Beach Boys* (1966).

"We Are The Champions/We Will Rock You" is released by *Queen* (1977).

October 23

Born: Johnny Carson (1925)
Ellie Greenwich (1939)

Pelé (1940)
Greg Ridley, *Spooky Tooth* (1941)

Died: Al Jolson (1950)

Tommy Edwards (1969)

Events: "Quarter to Three" by Gary U.S. Bonds is released (1960).

John F. Kennedy orders the blockade of Cuba (1962).

Pippin opens on Broadway (1972).

October 24

Born: Sonny Terry (1911)
J.P. "The Big Bopper" Richardson (1930)
Bill Wyman [William Perks] (1939)

Ted Templeman [producer] (1944)
Jerry Edmonton, *Steppenwolf* (1946)
Dale "Buffin" Griffin, *Mott the Hoople* (1948)

Events: Dutch Schultz [Arthur Flegenheimer] shot by FBI (1935).

The Beatles start their first Scandinavian tour in Sweden (1963).

October 25

Born: Johann Strauss (1825)
Pablo Picasso (1881)
Admiral Richard Byrd (1888)

Helen Reddy (1942)
Jon Anderson, *Yes* (1944)

Died: Geoffrey Chaucer [poet] (1406)

Nick Drake [drug overdose] (1974)

Events: *The Rolling Stones* appear on "The Ed Sullivan Show" (1964).

October 26

Born: Mahalia Jackson (1911)
Maggie Roche, *The Roches* (1951)

Keith Strickland, *B-52's* (1953)

Died: Pablo Picasso (1975)

Events: John F. Kennedy gets Martin Luther King out of jail after a sit-in arrest (1960).

Bob Dylan plays Carnegie Hall (1963).

The first issue of *The Village Voice* hits the stands (1965).

The Beatles go to Buckingham Palace to get MBE, but first they smoke a joint in the bathroom (1965).

October 27

Born:

Teddy Roosevelt (1858)
Emily Post (1872)
Dylan Thomas (1914)
Cleo Laine (1927)
Floyd Cramer (1933)

Phillip Catherine (1942)
Garry Tallent, *E Street Band* (1949)
Simon LeBon, *Duran Duran* (1958)

Events:

The New York subway opens (1904).

Charles Manson's defense announces they'll call *The Beatles* to testify on certain meanings of their songs (1970).

Bruce Springsteen is featured on the covers of *Time* and *Newsweek* (1975).

October 28

Born:

Edith Head (1907)
James Cook [discoverer of Hawaii] (1728)
Dr. Jonas Salk [discoverer of the polio vaccine] (1914)

Charlie Daniels (1936)
Randy Newman (1943)
Wayne Fontana (1945)
Ricki Lee Reynolds, *Black Oak Arkansas* (1948)

Events:

Brian Epstein, a record store owner, is asked about "My Bonnie" by *The Beatles* released in Germany. He gets a few copies, goes to see them, and...(1961).

October 29

Born:

Zoot Sims (1925)
Denny Laine, *Wings* (1944)

Peter Green, ex-*Fleetwood Mac* (1946)

Died: Duane Allman [motorcycle accident] (1971)

Events:

The stock market crashes (1929).

Hair opens at The Public Theater, Greenwich Village (1967).

"Bat Out Of Hell" by Meat Loaf is released (1977).

John DeLorean is indicted on charges of conspiring to distribute cocaine worth an estimated $24 million to save his failing sports car company from bankruptcy (1982).

October 30

Born: Ezra Pound [American poet]   Grace Slick (1939)
       (1884)   Timothy B. Schmidt, *The Eagles*
      Charles Atlas (1893)   (1947)
      Eddie Holland (1939)

Events: Bob Dylan's *Rolling Thunder Revue* opens their tour in Plymouth,
Massachusetts (1975).

October 31

Born: John Keats (1795)   Russ Ballard, *Argent* (1947)
      Chiang Kai-shek (1887)   Bernard Edwards (1952)
      Ethel Waters (1900)   Larry Mullen, *U-2* (1961)
      Dale Evans (1912)   Tom Paxton (1937)
      Kinky Friedman (1944)   Annabella Lwin, *Bow Wow
                                    Wow* (1952)

Events: Halloween

"The War of the Worlds" is broadcast and sounds so real that many
were unable to tell it wasn't (1938).

"Bohemian Rhapsody" by *Queen* is released, their biggest hit (1975).

Melissa
Manchester

NOVEMBER

November 1

Born: Rick Grech, *Blind Faith* (1945)

Events: *The Beatles* begin a fourteen-day gig at the Star Club in Hamburg (1963).

The *Rolling Stones'* first hit, "I Wanna Be Your Man" b/w "Stoned," charts (1963).

Wham-O files patent for the Frisbee (1963).

"Wonderwall Music" by George Harrison is the first solo album by a Beatle (1968).

"Abbey Road," the final *Beatles* LP, is released (1969).

"Sergeant Pepper" is released in UHQR half speed by Mobile Fidelity, 5,000 quantity at $50. They sell out in two weeks (1982).

November 2

Born: Daniel Boone (1734)   Keith Emerson, *Emerson, Lake*
Marie Antoinette (1755)   *and Palmer* (1944)
Warren G. Harding (1865)   Goldie Hawn (1945)
Burt Lancaster (1913)   Dave Pegg, *Fairport*
Jay Traynor, *Jay and the*   *Convention* (1947)
  Americans (1938)

Events: *The Beatles* play for the Queen. John asks the "cheap seats to clap, those in the rich section, just rattle your jewelry" (1963).

"Peggy Sue," Buddy Holly's first hit, charts (1957).

"Maybelline" is released, Chuck Berry's first hit (1955).

"Rock Around The Clock" charts, Bill Haley's first hit (1955).

November 3

Born: James Reston (1909)   Lulu [Marie McDonald
Brian Poole, *The Tremolos* (1941)   McLaughlin Lawrie] (1948)
Doug Simper, *Deep Purple* (1946)   Adam Ant (1954)

Events: Stanley finds Livingston (1871).

Carly Simon and James Taylor wed (1972).

November 4

Born: Will Rogers (1879)
Walter Cronkite (1916)
Art Carney (1918)

Chris Difford, *Squeeze* (1954)
James Honeywell-Scott, *The Pretenders* (1956)

Events: Bob Dylan gives his first "uptown" New York City show at Chapter Hall in Carnegie Hall. Attendance is low, and the show loses money (1961).

Cream gives their last American concert in Providence, Rhode Island (1968).

The United States Embassy in Teheran, Iran, is occupied by several hundred lunatic students (1979).

November 5

Born: Roy Rogers (1912)
Vivien Leigh (1913)
Ike Turner (1931)
Art Garfunkel (1942)

Graham Parsons (1946)
Peter Noone, *Herman's Hermits* (1947)

November 6

Born: John Philip Sousa (1854)
Ray Conniff (1916)
Mike Nichols (1931)
P.J. Proby [James Marcus Smith] (1938)

Doug Sahm (1942)
George Young, *Flash In The Pan* (1947)
Glenn Frey, *Eagles* (1948)

Died: Billy Murcia, *New York Dolls* [choked to death] (1972)

November 7

Born: Madame Curie (1867)
Al Hirt (1922)
Joan Sutherland (1929)
Mary Travers, *Peter, Paul and Mary* (1937)

Dee Dee Clark (1938)
Johnny Rivers (1942)
Joni Mitchell (1943)
Nick Gilder (1951)

Died: Steve McQueen [cancer] (1980)

Events: Nixon loses California's gubernatorial election and tells us, "You won't have Richard Nixon to kick around any more" (1962).

Steve Anderson of Los Angeles plays the guitar nonstop for 114 hours, 17 minutes to set a new world record (1975).

November 8

Born: Katharine Hepburn (1907)   Bonnie Raitt (1949)
Patti Page (1927)   Larry Burnette, *Firefall* (1951)
Bonnie Bramlett (1927)   Terry De Miall Harron, *Adam
Roy Wood (1948)   and the Ants* (1958)

Died: Ivory Joe Hunter (1974)

Events: Cecil B. DeMille's seventieth and final flick, the sound remake of *The
Ten Commandments*, opens (1956).

Kennedy/Johnson defeat Nixon/Lodge in the closest election since
1884 (1960).

John and Cynthia Lennon divorce (1968).

November 9

Born: Ed Wynn (1886)   Lee Graziano, *American Breed*
Sargent Shriver (1915)   (1943)
Spiro T. Agnew (1918)   Alan Gratzer, *REO
Tom Fogerty, *Creedence   Speedwagon* (1948)
    Clearwater Revival* (1941)

Events: Brian Epstein sees *The Beatles* for the first time at the Cavern Club
(1961).

"Louie, Louie" by *The Kingsmen* charts (1963).

The first issue of *Rolling Stone* hits the stands with John Lennon on
the cover (1967).

Sugar Ray Leonard retires from boxing [junior middleweight and
welterweight champ] after an eye injury in training. He earned $40
million (1982).

November 10

Born: Tommy Dorsey (1905)   Tim Rice, composer of *Jesus
Richard Burton (1925)   Christ Superstar* (1944)
Tommy Facenda (1939)   Greg Lake, *Emerson, Lake
Screaming Lord Sutch (1940)   and Palmer* (1948)

Events: Kate Smith sings "God Bless America" for the first time in public on
Armistice Day over the radio (1938).

Bill Graham rents the Fillmore in San Francisco for $60.00 (1965).

The *Edmund Fitzgerald* sinks (1975).

November 11

Born: Senator William Proxmire (1915)
Kurt Vonnegut (1922)
Jonathan Winters (1925)
Mose Allison (1927)
LaVern Baker (1928)
Jesse Colin Young (1944)
Vince Martell, *Vanilla Fudge* (1945)
Chris Dreja, *The Yardbirds* (1946)
Pat "Dirty" Daugherty, *Black Oak Arkansas* (1947)

Died: Berry Oakley [motorcycle crash] (1972)

Events: World War I ends (1918).

Tarantula, Bob Dylan's book, is published (1970).

"American Prayer" by *The Doors* is released (1978).

November 12

Born: Bukka White (1934)
Bob Crewe (1931)
Brian Hyland (1943)
Jimmy Hayes, *The Persuasions* (1943)
Booker T. Jones (1944)
Neil Young (1945)

Events: Loggins and Messina release "Finale," their last LP (1977).

November 13

Born: Robert Louis Stevenson (1850)
John Hammond, Jr. (1942)
Terry Reid (1949)

Events: Pablo Casals plays at the White House (1961).

Queen's "Jazz" tour starts in Boston (1978).

November 14

Born: Mamie Eisenhower (1896)
Freddie Garrity, *Freddie And The Dreamers* (1940)
Stephen Bishop (1951)

Died: Keith Reif, *The Yardbirds* [electrocuted onstage] (1976)

November 15

Born: Mantovani (1905) Clyde McPhatter (1933)
Petula Clark (1932) Dave Clark (1942)

Events: *Love Me Tender,* starring Elvis Presley, opens in New York City at the Paramount Theatre (1956).

Janis Joplin is busted for using vulgar and indecent language in Tampa (1969).

Elvis Costello opens his first United States tour at the Old Waldorf in San Francisco (1977).

November 16

Born: W.C. Handy (1873) Toni Brown, *Joy of*
Burgess Meredith (1909) *Cooking* (1938)

Died: Clark Gable (1960) Sam Rayburn (1961)

Events: "Great Balls of Fire" by Jerry Lee Lewis is released (1957).

"With A Little Help From My Friends: by Joe Cocker charts (1968).

November 17

Born: Rock Hudson (1925) Gene Clark, *The Byrds* (1941)
Gordon Lightfoot (1938) Tom Seaver (1944)

November 18

Born: Eugene Ormandy (1889) Kim Wilde (1960)
Hank Ballard (1936) Kirk Hammett, Metallica (1962)

Died: Junior Parker [during brain Danny Whitten [drug overdose]
operation] (1971) (1972)

Events: The Gettysburg Address is delivered by Abraham Lincoln (1863).

Richard Hell and the Voidoids premiere at CBGB in New York City (1976).

The *B-52s* debut LP goes gold (1980).

November 19

Born: Indira Gandhi (1917)
Roy Campanella (1921)
Ray Collins, *Mothers of Invention* (1937)

Dick Cavett (1938)
Fred Lipsius, *Blood, Sweat and Tears* (1944)
Matt Sorum, Guns N' Roses (1960)

Died: Joe Hill (1915)

Events: Sunday *New York World* becomes the first newspaper to print a color section (1893).

November 20

Born: Alistair Cooke (1908)
Emilio Pucci (1914)
Gene Tierney (1920)
Kaye Ballard (1926)
Dick Smothers (1938)
Norman Greenbaum (1942)

Dan McBride, *Sha Na Na* (1945)
Duane Allman (1946)
Joe Walsh, *The Eagles* (1947)
George Grantham, *Poco* (1947)
Gary Green, *Gentle Giant* (1950)

Died: Alan Sherman (1973)

Generalissimo Francisco Franco (1975)

Events: *Cabaret* opens on Broadway (1966).

November 21

Born: Marlo Thomas (1938)
David Porter (1940)
Dr. John [Mac Rebennack] (1940)

Alphonse Mouson (1948)
Lonnie Jordan, *War* (1948)
Livingston Taylor (1950)

Events: *The Beatles* release the "White Album" (1968).

On CBS-TV's "Dallas," J.R. is shot in the season's final episode. Thus begins a worldwide preoccupation over whodunit. The answer captures a 53.3 rating for the new season's premiere episode (1980).

Don Henley, drummer for *The Eagles,* is arrested at his home in Los Angeles for giving underaged girls cocaine and Quaaludes for sexual purposes (1980).

November 22

Born: Charles DeGaulle (1890)
Hoagy Carmichael (1899)
Geraldine Page (1924)
Steve Caldwell, *Orleans* (1942)
Billie Jean King (1943)

Aston "Family Man" Barrett,
The Wailers (1946)
Rod Price, *Foghat* (1947)
"Miami" Steve Van Zandt (1949)

Died: John F. Kennedy [assassinated] (1963)

Events: *Casablanca*, starring Humphrey Bogart, Ingrid Bergman, Peter Lorre, Sidney Greenstreet, Claude Rains, and Dooley Wilson, opens (1942).

November 23

Born: Billy "The Kid" Bonney (1859)
Boris Karloff (1887)
Harpo Marx (1893)

Charles Bronson (1922)
Cecil Hooker, *Snuff* (1950)
Bruce Hornsby (1954)

Died: Shemp Howard [The Three Stooges] (1955)

Events: The first jukebox is installed in the Paris Royal Hotel in San Francisco by the Pacific Phonograph Company (1899).

Life's first issue hits the streets (1936).

November 24

Born: Zachary Taylor (1784)
Henri de Toulouse-Lautrec
 (1864)
Scott Joplin (1868)
John V. Lindsay (1921)
William F. Buckley, Jr. (1925)
Gary Boyle, *Isotope* (1941)

Donald "Duck" Dunn, *Blues
 Brothers* (1941)
Robin Williamson, *The
 Incredible String Band* (1943)
Lee Michaels (1943)
Richard Tee (1943)
Bev Bevan, *ELO* (1944)

Died: Lee Harvey Oswald [assassinated] (1963)
Freddie Mercury, Queen (1991)

November 25

Born: Andrew Carnegie (1835)   Val Fuentes, *It's A Beautiful*
Joe DiMaggio (1914)   *Day* (1947)
Paul Desmond (1924)   J.J. Jackson, MTV Video Jock
Tina Turner (1941)   Linda LaFlamme (1947)
Roy Lynes, *Status Quo* (1943)

Died: Hugh Moore [Dixie Cup inventor] (1972)

Events: Miles Davis plays his first recording session with Charlie Parker (1945).

Bill Haley's "Rock Around The Clock" becomes the first rock song to hit No. 1 in the United Kingdom (1955).

John Lennon returns his MBE to the Queen in protest of the involvement in Vietnam and Biafra (1969).

"The Last Waltz" is *The Band*'s farewell show at Winterland, San Francisco (1976).

November 26

Born: Eric Sevareid (1912)   John McVie, *Fleetwood*
Charles Schulz (1922)   *Mac* (1945)
Robert Goulet (1933)   Burt Reiter, *Focus* (1946)

Died: Tommy Dorsey (1956)

Events: *Thoroughbreds Don't Cry,* the first movie starring Judy Garland and Mickey Rooney, opens (1937).

Cream plays its farewell concert at London's Royal Albert Hall (1969).

November 27

Born: Al Jackson, *Booker T. & The*   Randy Brecker (1945)
M.G.'s (1935)   Kevin Kavanaugh, *Asbury*
Bruce Lee (1940)   *Jukes* (1951)
Jimi Hendrix [James Marshal
Hendrix] (1942)

Events: Ken Kesey hosts the first Acid Test (1965).

Grease opens on Broadway and becomes the longest-running show ever (1972).

November 28

Born:
William Blake (1757)
Berry Gordy, Jr. [founder of Motown Records) (1929)
Gato Barbieri (1934)

Randy Newman (1943)
Hugh McKenna, *Alex Harvey Band* (1949)

Events: John Lennon pays a £150 fine for possession of pot (1968).

November 29

Born:
Louisa May Alcott (1832)
Adam Clayton Powell (1908)
John Mayall (1933)
Meco (1939)
Chuck Mangione (1940)

Dennis Doherty, *The Mamas and the Papas* (1941)
Felix Cavaliere, *The Rascals* (1944)
Barry Goudreau, *Boston* (1951)

Died: Natalie Wood [drowned] (1981)

Events: "Two Virgins," the LP with a nude photo of John and Yoko, is released (1968).

November 30

Born:
Jonathan Swift (1667)
Mark Twain [Samuel Langhorne Clemens] (1825)
Winston Churchill (1874)
Allan Sherman (1924)
Dick Clark (1929)
G. Gordon Liddy (1930)
Abbie Hoffman (1936)

Paul Stookey, *Peter, Paul and Mary* (1937)
Leo Lyons, *Ten Years After* (1943)
Shuggie Otis (1954)
Billy Idol (1955)
Paul Young (1955)

Events: "At The Hop," by Danny and the Juniors, charts (1957).

*Mike
Oldfield*

*Jack
Bruce*

DECEMBER

December 1

Born: Mary Martin (1913)
Billy Paul (1934)
Lou Rawls (1935)
Woody Allen (1935)
Sandy Nelson (1938)
Lee Trevino (1939)

John Paul Densmore, *The
Doors* (1944)
Bette Midler (1945)
Gilbert O'Sullivan (1946)
Jaco Pastorius, *Weather Report*
(1951)

Events: *Promises, Promises* opens (1968).

"Magical Mystery Tour" is released by *The Beatles* (1967).

Gerald Casale, *Devo*, tells audience in Houston, "The men with badges want to take us to jail; so, we need to clear the aisles so the little piggies don't take Devo away." A riot allows *Devo* to finish the last fifteen minutes of the show (1982).

December 2

Born: Tom McGuiness, *McGuiness-Flint* (1941)

Events: *Taj Mahal* plays for death-row inmates in Washington State Penitentiary (1971).

"Wanted: Dead or Alive," Richard Pryor's LP, is released (1978).

Barney Clark is the recipient of the first plastic heart in Utah (1982).

December 3

Born: Andy Williams (1928)   Ozzy Osbourne (1948)

Died: Marty Feldman [stroke] (1982)

Events: Million-Dollar Quartet: Elvis, Jerry Lee Lewis, Johnny Cash, and Carl Perkins record at Sun, but the LP is never released (1956).

Camelot starring Richard Burton and Julie Andrews opens on Broadway (1960).

"My Aim Is True" is released, Elvis Costello's first LP (1977).

Tommy Steele donates Eleanor Rigby statue to Liverpool. Home movies of *The Beatles* are bought in a rummage sale for 80¢ (1982).

December 4

Born:
Lillian Russell (1861)
Freddy Cannon (1940)
Chris Hillman, *The Byrds* (1942)
Dennis Wilson, *The Beach Boys* (1944)

Southside Johnny Lyon (1948)
Gary Rossington, *The Rossington-Collins Band* (1951)

Died:
Tommy Bolin, *Deep Purple* (1976)

Eleven people are trampled trying to get through three open doors to a general admission concert by *The Who* at the Riverfront Coliseum in Cincinnati (1979).

Events:
Bob Marley is shot at his Jamaican home along with his manager and a member of *The Wailers* (1976).

December 5

Born:
General George Custer (1839)
Walt Disney (1901)
Otto Preminger (1906)
Little Richard (1932)

J. J. Cale (1938)
John Cale (1940)
Jim Messina (1947)

Events:
Prohibition is repealed (1933).

The Beatles open the Apple Boutique (1968).

"Beggar's Banquet" by *The Rolling Stones* is released; they throw one to celebrate (1968).

December 6

Born:
Ira Gershwin (1896)
Dave Brubeck (1920)
Mike Smith, *Dave Clark Five* (1943)

Jonathan King (1944)
Rick Bucker, *The Jam* (1955)

Died:
Huddie "Leadbelly" Ledbetter (1949)

Events:
Thomas Edison records the first words: "Mary had a little lamb" (1877).

The Rolling Stones concert at Altamont, California, results in the death of a fan by a Hells Angels beating, "protection for band" (1969).

Gimme Shelter, the *Stones'* flick, opens in New York City (1970).

WDVE-FM in Pittsburgh uses Hal, the talking computer (also the name of the computer in 2001) so sing a Christmas carol with a Donnie Iris record, "Hal's Christmas Wish." Hal sang the "Fa-la-la-la-la's" (1982).

December 7

Born: Eli Wallach (1915)   Tom Waits (1949)
           Harry Chapin (1942)

Events: "I Want To Hold Your Hand" enters the singles charts at No. 1 for
           The Beatles in United Kingdom (1963).

           Geraldine Keeling, a classical music scholar, wins UCLA's first $1,000
           John Lennon Award presentation that honors a graduate student
           whose research best exemplified Lennon's spirit. She uses the award
           to study Liszt in Europe (1982).

           Harry Chapin received Congressional Gold Medal. Only 116 persons
           awwarded it since George Washington for efforts to eliminate world
           hunger (posthumously)

December 8

Born: James Thurber (1894)   Jim [James Douglas] Morrison
           Jean Ritchie (1922)   (1943)
           Jimmy Smith (1925)   Graham Knight, *Marmalade*
           Sammy Davis, Jr. (1925)   (1946)
           Flip Wilson (1933)   Gregg Allman (1947)
           Jerry Butler (1939)

Died: John Lennon, the first rock assassination (1980).

Events: A printers' strike forces nine New York papers to close (1962).

           Frank Sinatra, Jr., is kidnapped at gunpoint from a Lake Tahoe
           motel, released after 34 hours (1963).

           Bob Dylan plays a benefit at Madison Square Garden for Rubin
           "Hurricane" Carter (1975).

           Public Image Ltd., the new band by Johnny Rotten (Johnny Lydon)
           premieres (1978).

December 9

Born: Douglas Fairbanks, Jr. (1909)
           Lee J. Cobb (1911)
           Kirk Douglas (1918)
           Jr. Wells (1932)
Sam Strain, *The Imperials* (1940)
Rick Danko, *The Band* (1943)
Joan Armatrading (1950)
Donny Osmond (1957)

Died: Marty Robbins [heart failure; country singer who recorded 500 songs,
           18 gold ones] (1982).

           Roy Orbison (1988).

December 10

Born: Emily Dickinson (1830)   Chad Stuart, *Chad and Jeremy*
              Arthur Rimbaud (1891)   (1943)
              Chet Huntley (1911)   Guru Maharaj Ji (1957)

Died: Otis Redding and three members of the *Bar-kays* in a plane crash (1967).

Events: *The Sex Pistols* record for Warner Bros. "Never Mind The Bollocks,
              Here's The Sex Pistols" (1977).

December 11

Born: Fiorello LaGuardia (1882)   Brenda Lee (1944)
              Big Mama Thornton (1920)   Jermaine Jackson (1954)
              David Gates (1939)

Died: Sam Cooke [shot by mistake] (1964)

December 12

Born: Edward G. Robinson (1893)   Tony Williams (1945)
              Frank [Francis Albert] Sinatra   Clive Bunker, *Jethro Tull* (1946)
                 (1917)   Jeff Lynne, *ELO* (1947)
              Connie Francis (1938)   Miroslav Vitous (1947)
              Dionne Warwick (1941)   Paul Rodgers, *Bad Company*
              Mike Pinder, *The Moody Blues*   (1949)
                 (1942)   Neil Part, *Rush* (1952)
              Dickie Betts, *The Allman*   Sheila E. (1959)
                 Brothers (1943)

Events: The first transatlantic radio signals are transmitted and received by
              Marconi (1901).

              "Promised Land" by Chuck Berry is released (1964).

              Mick Taylor leaves *The Rolling Stones* (1974).

              "The River" by Bruce Springsteen goes platinum (1980).

              "Zenyata Mondatta" by *The Police* goes gold (1980).

December 13

Born: Dick Van Dyke (1925)   Davey O'List, ex-*Roxy Music*
              Christopher Plummer (1927)   (1950)
              Tony Gomez, *The Foundations*
                 (1940)

Events: The first sound film is shown by Dr. Lee DeForest (1923).

              "Alice's Restaurant" by Arlo Guthrie is released (1969).

December 14

Born: Charlie "Silver Fox" Rich (1932)   Patty Duke (1946)
Joyce Vincent, *Dawn* (1946)

Died: Dinah Washington [drug overdose] (1963)

Events: "Hey Schoolgirl" is released, Neil Sedaka's first hit (1957).

"The Diary" is Tom & Jerry's [*Simon and Garfunkel*] first release (1958).

Yoko asks for ten minutes of silence worldwide at 2:00 p.m. Eastern time, in memory of John and all the love he presented to the world (1980).

December 15

Born: John "The Ear" Hammond (1910)   Dave Clark, *Dave Clark Five*
Allan "Rock 'N' Roll" Freed   (1942)
  (1922)   Carmine Appice (1946)
Cindy Birdsong, *The Supremes*   Paul Simonon, *Clash* (1955)
  (1939)

Died: Fats Waller [alcohol overdose]   Walt Disney (1966)
  (1943)
Glenn Miller [plane crash] (1944)

Events: The Bill of Rights is passed (1791).

Thomas Alva Edison files the patent for the phonograph (1877).

December 16

Born: Ludwig van Beethoven (1770)   John Abercrombie (1944)
Noel Coward (1899)   Tony Hicks, *The Hollies* (1945)
Margaret Mead (1901)   Benny Andersson, *Abba* (1946)
Joe Farrell (1937)

Events: The Boston Tea Party (1773).

The Wright brothers, Orville and Wilbur, fly the first powered, heavier-than-air craft at Kitty Hawk, North Carolina (1903).

John Schear has his first concert at The Capitol Theatre in Passaic, NJ, starring *The J. Geils Band* and *Humble Pie* (1971).

United National Records of Gary, Indiana, files a class-action suit against the top twelve record companies for "imposing general industrywide terms and conditions of sale upon their customers... inconsistent with free price competition" (1982).

December 17

Born:
Arthur Fiedler (1894)
Tommy Steele (1936)
Eddie Kendricks (1939)
Maurice White, *Earth, Wind & Fire* (1941)

Paul Butterfield (1942)
Jim Bonfanti, *Raspberries* (1948)
Charlie Barrett, *The Wailers* (1950)

Events:
Lynette "Squeaky" Fromme is sentenced to life in prison for the attempted assassination of President Gerald Ford (1975).

The Who play their farewell concert in Toronto before 15,000 fans. A pay TV hookup around North America allows an additional 5 million to see the show and hear it simulcast live over FM radio stations in dozens of markets (1982).

December 18

Born:
Ty Cobb (1886)
Betty Grable (1916)
Eddie Vinson (1917)
Chas Chandler, *The Animals* (1938)

Keith Richard (1943)
Bobby Keyes (1943)

Events:
The Rolling Stones broadcast a live concert over cable TV from Hampton, Virginia (1981).

December 19

Born:
Professor Longhair (1918)
David Susskind (1920)
Phil Ochs (1940)
Maurice White, *Earth, Wind & Fire* (1941)
Alvin Lee, *Ten Years After* (1944)

Zal Yanovsky, *Lovin' Spoonful* (1944)
John McEuen, *The Dirt Band* (1945)
Lenny White (1949)

Events:
Ron Wood is named as the new second guitarist for *The Rolling Stones* (1975).

December 20

Born:
Bobby Colomby, *Blood Sweat and Tears* (1944)

Peter Criss, *Kiss* (1947)

Died:
Bobby Darin [during heart surgery] (1973)

Events:
Elvis gets his Army induction notice (1957).

"The Girl is Mine" by Paul McCartney becomes the first 45 released since 1977 in Israel. Michael Jackson shares the vocals on the record, which is released for some reason on yellow vinyl (1982).

December 21

Born: Joseph Stalin (1879)
Jane Fonda (1937)
Carl Wilson, *The Beach Boys* (1946)

Frank [Francis Vincent] Zappa (1940)
Chris Evert-Lloyd (1954)

Events: Pilgrims land (1620).

"Ramblin' Gamblin' Man" charts, Bob Seger's first hit (1968).

The *Apollo Eight* space shot (1968).

Crosby, Stills and Nash begin their musical partnership in Los Angeles (1968).

December 22

Born: Lady Bird Johnson (1912)
Robin Gibb, *The Bee Gees* (1949)

Maurice Gibb, *The Bee Gees* (1949)

Died: Ma Rainey (1939)

Events: "Telstar," by *The Tornadoes,* becomes the first record by an English band to hit No. 1 on the charts in the United States (1962).

A Japanese department store pays $23,595 for the old record awarded *The Beatles* for "Sergeant Pepper" in a Sotheby auction (1982).

MTV broadcasts the world premiere of Bruce Springsteen's first video, a black-and-white clip of Atlantic City, based on the song of the same title. Springsteen doesn't appear in the clip but approved it (1982).

December 23

Born: "Little" Esther Phillips (1935)
Johnny Kidd (1939)
Tim Hardin (1940)
Jorma Kaukonen, *Hot Tuna* (1940)
Ronald Busby, *Iron Butterfly* (1945)

Luther Grosvenor, *Spooky Tooth* (1949)
Johnny Contardo, *Sha Na Na* (1951)

Died: Charles Atlas (1973)

Jack "Just the facts, Ma'am" Webb of "Dragnet" fame, from heart failure (1982)

Events: "Ready, Steady, Go" final episode is broadcast on BBC (1966).

"Foxy Lady" by Jimi Hendrix is released (1967).

Rod Stewart donates all the money he earns from "Do You Think I'm Sexy?" to UNICEF. This song is his biggest hit ever (1978).

December 24

Born: Kit Carson (1809)
Howard Hughes (1905)
Cab Calloway (1907)
Lee Dorsey (1924)
Ava Gardner [Lucy Johnson]
(1924)

Jan Akkerman, *Focus* (1946)
Ian Burden, *Human League*
(1957)

Events: "Rocket To Russia" by *The Ramones* charts (1977).

"Starting Over" goes gold for John Lennon (1980).

December 25

Born: Jesus Christ
Clara Barton (1821)
Humphrey Bogart (1899)
Billy Horton, *Silhouettes* (1937)
Bob James (1939)
O'Kelly Isley (1939)
Henry Vestine, *Canned Heat*
(1944)

Noel Redding, *The Jimi Hendrix*
Experience (1945)
Trevor Lucas, *Fairport*
Convention (1945)
Jimmy Buffett (1946)
Annie Lenox (1954)

Died: W.C. Fields (1946)

Events: Paul McCartney and Jane Asher announce their engagement (1967).

December 26

Born: Rose Mary Woods (1917)
Steve Allen (1921)
Alan King (1927)
Phil Spector (1939)

Ernie Cate, *Cate Brothers*
(1942)
Earl Cate, *Cate Brothers* (1942)
Lars Ulrich, Metallica (1963)

Events: Fidel Castro lands on Cuba with a band of soldiers to begin the revolution (1956).

The movie *Magical Mystery Tour,* by *The Beatles,* premieres on BBC-TV, in black and white (1967).

Concerts for Kampuchea, starring several of the top acts in the United Kingdom, is held in Hammersmith Odeon, London, for the benefit of hungry children (1979).

The personal home computer is named *Time* magazine's "Man of the Year." Runners-up are Menachem Begin, Margaret Thatcher, Paul Volker, and E.T. (1982).

December 27

Born: Marlene Dietrich (1901)
Pete Brown (1940)
Leslie McGuire, *The Pacemakers* (1941)
Michael Pinder, *The Moody Blues* (1941)

Pete Quaife, *Kinks* (1943)
Tracy Nelson (1944)
Mick Jones, *Foreigner* (1947)

Died: Bert Berns [producer, heart attack] (1967)

Hoagy Carmichael [composer, heart attack] (1981)

Events: Radio City Music Hall opens (1932).

December 28

Born: Woodrow Wilson (1856)
Earl "Fatha" Hines (1905)
Sam Levenson (1911)
Roebuck "Pops" Staples (1915)
John Otis (1924)

Dorsey Burnette (1932)
Bobby Comstock (1943)
Edgar Winter (1947)
Alex Chilton, *The Boxtops* (1950)

Died: Dennis Wilson, *The Beach Boys* [drowned] (1983)

Events: "Tutti Fruitti" by Little Richard charts (1955).

December 29

Born: Pablo Casals (1876)
Mary Tyler Moore (1937)
Jon Voight (1938)

Ray Thomas, *The Moody Blues* (1942)
Yvonne Elliman (1951)

Died: Tim Hardin [drug overdose] (1980)

December 30

Born: Rudyard Kipling (1865)
Bo Diddley [Ellis McDaniels] (1928)
Andy Williams (1930)
Jack Lord (1930)

Skeeter Davis (1931)
Sandy Koufax (1935)
Del Shannon (1939)
Davy Jones, *The Monkees* (1946)

Died: Richard Rodgers (1979)

Events: *Emerson, Lake and Palmer* announce their official breakup (1979).

December 31

Born: Odetta (1930)
Andy Summers, *Police* (1942)
John Denver (1943)
Patti Smith (1946)

Burton Cummings (1947)
Donna Summer (1948)
Tony Hamilton, *Aerosmith*
(1948)

Died: Rick Nelson [plane crash] (1985)

Events: *The Beach Boys* give their first show with that name; they were *Carl and The Passions* (1961).

Jimi Hendrix and Band of Gypsies [Buddy Miles and Billy Cox] premiere at the Fillmore East and release a live LP of the show which is regarded as one of the best ever (1969).

"Rock of Ages" by *The Band* is recorded at The New York Academy of Music. Bob Dylan joins for the encore, but this doesn't make the double LP (1971).

MTV hosts its First New Year's Eve Bash with *Bow Wow Wow*, Karla DeVito, and David Johansen (1981).

The $15,000 electronic news ribbon in Times Square is lit for the first time since 1977 when it was cut off because it cost too much. The first message at 5:00 p.m. said "Happy Holidays New York" (1982).

MTV holds Second Annual New Year's Eve Bash with *Duran Duran, A Flock of Seagulls, The Producers,* and *Jack Mack and the Heart Attack* (1982).

Miami Steve Van Zandt weds Maureen Santoro in New York City's Harkness House. Little Richard performs the ceremony with Bruce Springsteen as best man. Little Milton and Gary U.S. Bonds perform at the reception (1982).

Paul "Ace"
Frehley

Ringo
Starr

Donovan

*Dave
Mason*

Joe
Cocker

Tina
Turner

*Paul
McCartney*

INDEX

B

Lauren Bacall 9/16, 10/11, 11/22
Barbara Bach 4/27
Johann Sebastian Bach 3/21
Burt Bacharach 5/12
Randy Bachman 9/27
Robbie Bachman 2/18
Joan Baez 1/9, 3/9, 8/17, 9/12
Pearl Bailey 3/29
Philip Bailey 5/8
Carroll Baker 5/28
Ginger Baker 8/19, 7/16
Joseph Baker 6/3
LaVern Baker 11/11
Lenny Baker 4/18
Balboa 9/12
Long John Baldry 1/12
Marty Balin 1/30, 7/6
David Ball 3/30, 5/3
Hank Ballard 11/18
Lucille Ball 5/4, 8/6
Florence Ballard 6/30
Kaye Ballard 11/20
Russ Ballard 10/31
Anne Bancroft 9/17
The Band 7/28, 8/21, 11/25, 12/31
Band of Gypsies 12/31
Bangladesh 7/21, 7/31
Lester Bangs 4/30
Barbie 3/1
Gato Barbieri 11/28
Brigitte Bardot 9/28
Barriemore Barlow 9/10
Bar-kays 12/10
P.T. Barnum 4/7, 7/5
Clive Barnes 5/13
Paul Barrere 7/3
Aston Barrett 11/22
Charlie Barrett 12/17
Syd Barrett 1/6
Gene Barry 6/14
Jeff Barry 4/3
John Barrymore 2/15
Lionel Barrymore 4/28
Jack Bartley 5/16
Clara Barton 12/25
Count Basie 8/21
Shirley Bassey 1/8
Batman 1/13
Skip Batten 2/2
Ronnie Band 5/4
Joe Bauer 9/26
"Bowser" Bauman 9/14
Anne Baxter 5/7

Warner Baxter 1/20
Beach Boys 2/17, 4/1, 7/3, 10/22, 12/31
Beatles 1/1, 1/12, 1/14, 1/20, 1/24, 1/30,
   2/1, 2/2, 2/3, 2/4, 2/7, 2/8, 2/9, 2/11,
   2/12, 2/14, 2/22, 2/25, 3/14, 3/16,
   3/21, 4/9, 5/1, 5/9, 5/18, 6/1, 6/6,
   6/9, 6/10, 6/12, 6/15, 7/6, 7/29, 7/30,
   8/4, 8/5, 8/16, 8/19, 8/23, 8/27, 8/28,
   8/29, 8/30, 9/20, 10/1, 10/5, 10/18,
   10/24, 10/26, 10/28, 11/1, 11/2, 11/9,
   11/21, 12/1, 12/3, 12/5, 12/7, 12/16,
   12/22, 12/26
Warren Beatty 3/30
Jeff Beck 6/24, 10/16
Joe Beck 7/7
Walter Becker 2/20, 6/11
Gary Beckley 9/12
Captain Beefheart 1/15
Ludwig van Beethoven 12/16
Be-In 1/14
Bix Beiderbecke 3/10
Harry Belafonte 3/1
Alexander Graham Bell 3/3, 3/7
Archie Bell 9/1
Maggie Bell 1/11
John Belushi 1/24, 3/5
Pat Benatar 1/10, 2/20
Tony Benedetto 8/3
Estelle Bennet 7/22
Marc Benno 7/1
Jack Benny 2/14
George Benson 3/2
Brook Benton 9/19
Candice Bergen 5/8
Edgar Bergen 2/16
Ingmar Bergman 7/14
Ingrid Bergman 8/29, 11/22
Irving Berlin 5/11
Emile Berliner 9/26
Sarah Bernhardt 10/22
Bert Berns 12/27
Leonard Bernstein 8/25
Yogi Berra 5/12
Valerie Bertinelli 4/11
Chuck Berry 1/15, 4/19, 6/11 10/18,
   11/2, 12/12
Jan Berry 4/3, 4/12
Pete Best 8/16
Plastic Bertrand 8/26
Dickie Betts 12/12
Bev Bevan 11/24
Beverly Hillbillies 9/26
B-52s 11/18
Big Brother & The Holding Co. 7/25

Pat Burke 10/9
Raymond Burr 5/21
Pete Burrell 5/9
Richard Burton 11/10, 12/3
Trevor Burton 3/9
Ronald Busby 12/23
Kate Bush 7/30
Geezer Butler 7/17
Jerry Butler 12/8
Paul Butterfield 12/17
Red Buttons 2/5
Richard Byrd 10/25
The Byrds 1/14, 4/9, 5/15
David Byrne 5/14
Dave Byron 1/29
Lord Byron 1/22
Ed "Kookie" Byrnes 4/26, 7/30

C

Augustus Caesar 9/23
Julius Caesar 1/13, 3/15
Sid Caesar 9/8
Cabaret 2/13
Charlotte Caffey 10/21
Jimmy Cagney 1/2
Cal Jam 3/18
Steve Caldwell 11/22
Tommy Caldwell 5/30
J. J. Cale 12/5
John Cale 12/5
Cab Calloway 12/24
Al Capone 1/17
Truman Capote 9/30
Al Capp 9/28
Capricorn Records 1/27
Godfrey Cambridge 2/26
Camelot 12/3
Roy Campanella 11/19
Glen Campbell 4/10
Freddy Cannon 12/4
Jim Capaldi 2/8, 8/24
Capitol Records 4/1
Capitol Theatre 12/16
Carl and the Passions 12/31
George Carlin 5/12
Belinda Carlisle 8/17
Bun E. Carlos 6/12
Eric Carmen 8/11
Hoagy Carmichael 12/27
Andrew Carnegie 11/25
Carnegie Hall 5/5
Kim Carnes 7/20
Art Carney 11/4
Radio Caroline 3/28

Karen Carpenter 2/4
Richard Carpenter 10/15
LeRoy Carr 4/29
Lewis Carroll 7/4
Johnny Carson 10/25
Kit Carson 5/23, 12/23
Carlene Carter 5/18, 8/18
June Carter 6/23
Rubin "Hurricane" Carter 3/21
Ron Carter 3/4
Alan Cartwright 10/10
Enrico Caruso 2/25
Jack Casady 4/13
Pablo Casals 11/13, 12/29
Casanova 4/2
Johnny Cash 2/6, 4/17, 5/1, 6/7, 8/2,
    12/23
David Cassidy 4/12, 7/9, 8/14
Ed Cassidy 5/4
Fidel Castro 8/13, 12/26
Earl Cate 12/26
Ernie Cate 12/26
Phillip Catherine 10/27
Catherine the Great 5/2, 6/16
Felix Cavaliere 11/29
Cavern Club 1/16, 2/28, 3/21
Dick Cavett 11/19
Edgar Cayce 1/3, 3/18
CBS Records 1/8, 1/31, 3/2, 5/23, 6/17,
    6/21
Peter Cetera 5/20, 9/13
Richard Chamberlain 3/31
Wilt Chamberlain 8/12
George Chambers 9/22
Lester Chambers 4/13
Martin Chambers 9/4
Willie Chambers 3/2
Les Chadwick 5/11
Chas Chandler 12/18
Gene Chandler 1/13, 7/6
Lon Chaney 4/1, 9/2
Harry Chapin 7/16, 12/7
Charlie Chaplin 4/16, 10/15
Mark Chapman 8/24
Charlemagne 4/2
Ray Charles 9/23
Sam Chatman 2/2
Cesar Chavez 9/30
Geoffrey Chaucer 10/25
Paddy Chayefsky 1/29
Cheap Trick 9/10
Chubby Checker 1/14, 8/7, 10/3
Anton Chekhov 1/29
Cher 1/7, 4/3, 5/20, 6/26, 6/30, 7/10, 9/1

The Crickets 1/26
Peter Criss 12/20
Jim Croce 1/10, 9/20
Dash Crofts 8/14
Walter Cronkite 11/4
Steve Cropper 10/21
Bing Crosby 5/2, 9/28, 10/14
David Crosby 3/28, 8/14, 12/21
CSNY 7/9
Cuba 1/3, 1/31, 3/2, 5/1, 10/23, 12/26
Robert Culp 8/16, 9/5
Burton Cummings 12/31
George Cummings 7/28
Madame Curie 11/7
Chris Curtis 8/16
King Curtis 3/27, 8/13
Tony Curtis 6/3, 7/2
Cardinal Cushing 8/24
George Custer 6/25, 12/5

D
Steve Dahl 7/13
Richard Daley 5/15
Salvador Dali 5/11
Dallas 11/21
Roger Daltrey 3/1, 4/3
Jarry Dammers 5/22
Jim Dandy 3/30
Dino Danelli 7/23
Charlie Daniels 1/23, 10/28
Rick Danko 12/9
Danny and the Juniors 11/30
Dante 9/14
Bobby Darin 5/14, 7/22, 12/20
Dark Horse Records 9/6
James Darren 10/3
Charles Darwin 2/12
Pat Daugherty 11/11
Hal David 5/25
Lenny Davidson 5/30
Dave Davies 2/3
Ray Davies 1/29, 6/21
Richard Davies 7/22
Bette Davis 4/5
Clive Davis 5/23
Jefferson Davis 6/3
Paul Davis 4/20
Jefferson Davis 6/3
Miles Davis 5/25, 11/25
Sammy Davis, Jr. 12/8
Skeeter Davis 12/30
Spencer Davis 7/17
Doris Day 4/3, 11/8
John Deacon 8/19

James Dean 2/8
Jan & Dean 3/7, 6/15
Jimmy Dean 8/10
Kiki Dee 3/6
Daniel Defoe 2/1
Dee Deforest 12/13
Charles DeGaulle 11/22
Olivia deHavilland 7/1
Desmond Dekker 7/16
John DeLorean 10/29
Brad Delp 6/12
Cecil B. DeMille 8/12, 11/8
Sandy Denny 1/16
John Densmore 12/1
John Denver 12/31
Jack Dempsey 6/24
Derek & The Dominoes 8/10, 10/15
Jackie DeShannon 8/21
Jimmy Destri 4/13
Willie DeVille 8/27
Tommy DeVito 6/19
Devo 9/30, 12/1
Thomas Dewey 3/24
Neil Diamond 1/24, 5/21
Charles Dickens 2/7
Angie Dickinson 9/30
Emily Dickinson 12/10
Bo Diddley 12/30
Marlene Dietrich 12/27
Chris Difford 11/4
Doug Dillard 3/6
Phyllis Diller 7/17
John Dillinger 6/22, 7/22
Joe DiMaggio 11/25
Al DiMeola 7/22
Dion 7/18
Dire Straits 1/19
Walt Disney 2/3, 12/5, 12/15
Disneyland 7/17, 8/6
Willie Dixon 4/1
Dickie Do 6/17
Play-Doh 9/16
Dennis Doherty 11/29
Mickey Dolenz 3/9
Fats Domino 2/16, 2/27
Jerry Donahue 9/24
Doonesbury 1/1
The Doors 1/14, 7/7, 11/11
Lee Dorman 9/15
Jimmy Dorsey 2/29, 6/12
Lee Dorsey 12/24
Tommy Dorsey 11/10, 11/26
Neil Doughty 7/29
Greg Douglas 10/11

Barbara Feldon 9/18
Marty Feldman 12/3
Jose Feliciano 7/2, 9/8
Freddie Fender 2/15
Jay Ferguson 5/10
Brian Ferry 9/26
Arthur Fiedler 7/10, 12/17
James Fielder 10/4
W.C. Fields 4/9, 12/25
Fillmore Auditorium 1/3, 1/14, 5/16,
   6/27, 7/3, 12/31
Johnny Fingers 9/10
Bobby Fischer 3/9
Eddie Fisher 8/10, 9/26
Matt Fisher 3/7
Edmund Fitzgerald 9/24
Roberta Flack 2/10
Bob Flannigan 8/22
Lester Flatt 5/11, 6/28
Fleetwood Mac 5/20, 7/12, 8/12, 10/15
Mick Fleetwood 6/24
Peggy Fleming 7/27
Hughie Flint 3/15
Flintstones 9/30
Flock of Seagulls 12/31
Eddie Floyd 6/25
Errol Flynn 6/20, 10/14
Dan Fogelberg 8/13
John Fogerty 5/28
George Foreman 1/10
Henry Fonda 5/16
Jane Fonda 12/21
Peter Fonda 2/23
Wayne Fontana 10/28
Frankie Ford 8/4
Gerald Ford 12/17
Glenn Ford 5/1
Henry Ford 7/10
John Ford 3/5
Tennessee Ernie Ford 2/13
Foreigner 8/22
George Foreman 1/10
Bob Fosse 6/23
Stephen Foster 1/13, 7/4
The Four Seasons 8/24
Kim Fowley 7/27
Terry Fox 7/28
Peter Frampton 2/5, 4/22
Connie Francis 12/12
Aretha Franklin 3/25, 4/23
Benjamin Franklin 1/17, 4/17, 6/5
Chris Frantz 5/8
Andy Frazier 8/7
Smokin' Joe Frazier 1/12, 3/8

Walt Frazier 3/29
Stan Freberg 8/7
Allan Freed 1/20, 3/21, 12/15
Bobby Freeman 6/13
Ace Frehley 4/27
Sigmund Freud 5/6
Glenn Frey 11/6
Kinky Friedman 10/31
Robert Fripp 5/16
Frisbee 11/1
Craig Frost 4/20
Robert Frost 3/26
Val Fuentes 11/25
Jessie Fuller 1/30
Robert Fulton 1/30, 8/16
Annette Funicello 10/22
Funny Girl 3/26
Richie Furay 5/9

G

Clark Gable 1/9, 2/1, 11/16
Peter Gabriel 5/13
Paul Gadd 1/24
Steve Gadd 4/9
Ed Gagliardi 2/13
Steven Gaines 10/20
Rory Gallagher 3/2
Johnny Gamble 2/4
Indira Gandhi 11/19
Mahatma Gandhi 2/4
Greta Garbo 3/4, 9/18
Janice Garfat 3/3
Art Garfunkel 1/1, 3/30, 9/19, 11/5
Jerry Garcia 8/1
Ava Gardner 12/24
Bunk Gardner 5/2
Carl Gardner 4/29
James Garfield 7/2
Greddy Garity 11/14
Judy Garland 5/15, 6/10, 11/26
Errol Garner 6/15
Dave Garroway 7/13
Terri Garthwaite 7/11
David Gates 12/11
Marvin Gaye 4/2, 4/29
David Geffen 2/21
Lou Gehrig 6/19
Jerome Geils 2/20
Bob Geldof 9/14
Surgeon General 1/11
Genesis 4/4
Bobbie Gentry 7/27
Lowell George 6/29
Neil Geraldo 2/20

Jeff Hanna 8/11
Happening '68 1/6
Hard Day's Night 7/6
Tim Hardin 12/23, 12/29
Warren G. Harding 11/2
Roy Harper 6/12
Slim Harpo 1/11, 1/31
Richard Harris 10/1
Tim Harris 1/14
George Harrison 1/21, 1/27, 2/7, 2/25,
 7/27, 7/31, 8/29, 9/2, 9/6, 9/20, 11/1
Jerry Harrison 2/21
Mike Harrison 9/3
Rex Harrison 3/5
Wilbert Harrison 1/6
Terry De Miall Harron 11/8
Deborah Harry 7/1
William Hart 1/17
Alex Harvey 2/5
Sib Hashian 8/17
Bobby Hatfield 4/10
Donnie Hathaway 1/10, 1/13
Richie Havens 1/21
Coleman Hawkins 5/19
Dale Hawkins 8/22
Jay Hawkins 7/18
Ronnie Hawkins 1/10
Goldie Hawn 11/2
Bill Hayes 6/5, 11/12
Gabby Hayes 2/9
Helen Hayes 10/9
Isaac Hayes 8/6
Hayes Office 1/14
Justin Hayward 10/14
Rita Hayworth 10/17
Edith Head 10/28
Nicky Headon 5/30
Patricia Hearst 2/20, 3/20, 9/18
William Hearst 4/29
Hugh Hefner 4/9
Richard Hell 11/18
Hello Dolly 1/16
Levon Helm 5/26
Bobby Helms 8/15
Help 7/29
Ernest Hemingway 7/2, 7/21
Jimi Hendrix 1/3, 3/31, 4/1, 4/29, 6/24,
 6/29, 9/18, 9/21, 11/27, 12/23, 12/31
Nona Hendryx 8/18
Don Henley 7/22, 11/21
O. Henry 9/11
Patrick Henry 3/23, 5/29
Audrey Hepburn 2/5, 5/4
Katharine Hepburn 2/5, 11/8

Woody Herman 5/16
Carolyn Hester 9/29
Charlton Heston 10/24
Thor Heyerdahl 10/6
Nick Heyward 5/20
Tony Hicks 12/16
High Numbers 10/22
Dan Hill 6/3
Dave Hill 4/4
Joe Hill 11/19
Terry Hill 3/19
Edmund Hillary 7/20
Chris Hillman 12/4
Earl Hines 12/28
Hippies 10/6
Al Hirt 11/7
Alfred Hitchcock 4/19, 8/13
Bear Hite 2/26, 4/5
Dave Hlubek 8/24
Elsberry Hobbs 8/4
Randy Hobbs 3/22
Roger Hodgson 3/21
Abbie Hoffman 11/30
Dustin Hoffman 8/8
William Holden 4/17, 6/15
Noddy Holder 6/15
Brian Holland 2/15
Xaviera Hollander 2/14
Billie Holiday 4/7, 7/17
Buddy Holly 1/22, 1/24, 1/26, 2/3, 2/25,
 5/17, 9/7, 10/21, 11/2
Larry Holmes 6/11
Sherlock Holmes 1/6, 2/24
Oliver Wendell Holmes 3/8
Volker Homback 1/4
Homer 7/27, 8/7
James Honeywell-Scott 6/16
Cecil Hooker 11/22
John Lee Hooker 8/22
J. Edgar Hoover 1/1, 5/1
Bob Hope 5/29
Lightnin' Hopkins 1/30, 3/13
Mary Hopkins 5/3
Nicky Hopkins 2/24
Dennis Hopper 5/17
Hugh Hopper 4/29
Lena Horne 6/16
Marilyn Horne 1/16
Bruce Hornsby 11/23
Billy Horton 12/25
Johnny Horton 4/3
Hostages 1/20
Harry Houdini 3/24, 7/2
Robbie House 4/11

Kenny Jones 9/16
Mick Jones 6/26, 12/27
Paul Jones 2/24
Quincy Jones 3/14
Ricki Lee Jones 3/17
Shirley Jones 3/31
Steve Jones 5/3
Tom Jones 6/7
Janis Joplin 1/19, 2/14, 6/10, 7/12, 7/26,
   8/12, 10/4, 10/7, 11/15
Scott Joplin 4/1, 11/24
Lonnie Jordan 11/21
Journey 7/3
Jukebox 11/23
Bill Justis 10/14

K

Bert Kaempfert 10/16
Chiang Kai-shek 10/30
Kampuchea 12/26
Citizen Kane 5/1
Paul Kantner 3/12
Boris Karloff 11/23
Terry Kath 1/23
Steve Katz 5/9
Murray "The K" Kauffman 2/21
Irving Kaufman 10/9
Jorma Kaukonen 12/23
Kevin Kavanaugh 11/27
"Kaya" 4/22
John Kay 4/12
Howard Kaylan 6/22
Buster Keaton 10/4
John Keats 10/31
Ruby Keeler 8/25
Bob Keeshan 6/27
Helen Keller 6/27
Mike Kellie 3/24
Betty Kelly 8/23, 9/16
Gene Kelly 8/23
Grace Kelly 4/19
Eddie Kendricks 12/17
Ethel Kennedy 4/11
John F. Kennedy 1/20, 3/1, 3/23, 5/5,
   5/27, 9/26, 10/23, 10/26, 11/8, 11/22
Joseph Kennedy 9/6
Robert Kennedy 6/5
Rose Kennedy 7/22
Ted Kennedy 2/22
Stan Kenton 8/25
Jack Kerouac 10/21
Deborah Kerr 9/30
Doug Kershaw 1/24
Ken Kesey 7/27

Francis Scott Key 8/1
Bobby Keys 12/18
Steve Khan 4/23
Johnny Kidd 12/23
Jean-Claude Killy 8/30
Alan King 12/26
Albert King 4/25
B.B. King 9/16
Ben E. King 9/28
Billie Jean King 11/22
Carole King 2/9
Martin Luther King 1/15, 4/4, 8/28
Phil King 4/27
The Kingsmen 3/14, 11/9
The Kingston Trio 10/5
The Kinks 3/13, 9/26
Rudyard Kipling 12/30
Simon Kirke 8/27
Don Kirshner 4/17
Danny Kirwan 5/13
Kiss 10/14
John Klemmer 8/3
Earl Klugh 9/16
The Knack 8/3
Evel Knievel 10/17
Dave Knight 6/28
Gladys Knight 5/28
Graham Knight 12/8
Merald Knight 9/4
Stan Knight 2/12
Terry Knight 4/9
Mark Knopfler 8/12
Cub Koda 10/1
Al Kooper 2/5
Alexis Korner 4/19
Paul Kossof 3/19
Sandy Koufax 12/30
Ernie Kovaks 1/23
Billy J. Kramer 8/19
Bill Kreutzmann 6/7
Robbie Krieger 1/8
Kris Kristofferson 2/19, 6/22
Gene Krupa 1/15
Nikita Krushchev 4/17, 10/12

L

LaBamba 3/12
Patti LaBelle 5/24
David LaFlamme 4/5
Linda LaFlamme 11/25
Lafayette 9/6
LaGuardia 12/11
Cleo Laine 10/27
Denny Laine 10/29

Jeff Lynne 12/12
Loretta Lynn 4/14
Phil Lynnot 8/20
Lynyrd Skynyrd 10/20
Johnny Lyon 12/4
Leo Lyons 11/30

M

Ralph MacDonald 3/15
Hugh MacDowell 7/31
Ted Mack 10/4
Fred MacMurray 8/30
Madonna 8/16
Lester Maddox 9/30
Dolly Madison 8/24
James Madison 3/16
Johnny Maestro 5/7
Magical Mystery Tour 12/26
Taj Mahal 5/17, 12/2
Karl Malden 3/22
Gary Mallaber 10/11
Norman Mailer 1/31
The Mamas and the Papas 3/9
Mike Mainieri 7/24
Melissa Manchester 2/15
Henry Mancini 4/16
Ray Mancini 3/4
Harvey Mandel 3/11
Man from UNCLE 9/22
Chuck Mangione 11/29
Manhattan 5/24
Herbie Mann 4/16
Manfred Mann 9/5, 10/21
Jayne Mansfield 4/19
Charles Manson 3/6, 10/27
Mickey Mantle 10/20
Mantovani 11/15
Richard Manuel 4/3
Phil Manzanera 1/31
Ray Manzarek 2/12
Fredric March 8/31
Guglielmo Marconi 4/25, 12/12
Arif Mardin 3/15
Mariner IV 7/15
Bob Marley 2/5, 4/6, 5/11, 11/4, 12/4
Steve Marriott 1/30
Gerry Marsden 9/24
Marcel Marceau 3/22
E.G. Marshall 6/18
Vince Martell 11/11
Dean Martin 6/3, 6/7
Dewey Martin 9/30
George Martin 1/3, 2/11, 6/6
Mary Martin 12/1

Al Martino 10/7
Lee Marvin 2/19
Marx Brothers 10/20
Chico Marx 3/22
Groucho Marx 8/19, 10/2
Harpo Marx 11/23
Karl Marx 3/14, 5/5
M*A*S*H 1/14, 2/28, 9/17
Barbara Mason 8/9
Dave Mason 5/10
James Mason 5/15
Nick Mason 1/27
Mick Massi 9/19
Carlo Mastrangelo 10/5
Walter Matthau 10/1
Johnny Mathis 9/30
Glen Matlock 6/2, 8/27
Mattel 3/1
Brain May 7/19
Phil May 9/11
John Mayall 11/29
Augie Mayer 5/31
Curtis Mayfield 6/3
Willie Mays 5/6
MCA Records 1/30
Douglas McArthur 1/26, 8/14
Dan McBride 11/17
Eugene McCarthy 3/29
Jim McCarthy 7/25
Linda McCartney 2/3, 9/24
Mary McCartney 8/28
Paul McCartney 1/16, 1/31, 2/3, 2/15,
   3/8, 3/12, 6/15, 6/18, 7/20, 8/3, 8/10,
   8/29, 9/20, 9/23, 12/20, 12/25
Doug McClure 5/11
McCoys 8/14
Jimmy McCulloch 9/28
Danny McCullock 7/18
Ian McCullough 5/5
Country Joe McDonald 1/1
Ian McDonald 6/25
Jeannette McDonald 1/14, 6/18
Roddy McDowell 9/17
Spanky McFarlane 6/19
Frank McGhee 9/22
George McGovern 7/19
Craig McGregor 10/13
Roger McGuinn 5/29, 7/13
Tom McGuinness 12/1
Marry McGuire 10/15
Leslie McGuire 12/27
Robbie McIntosh 9/23
Goldie McJohn 5/2
Andy McKay 7/23

Hugh McKenna 11/28
Ted McKenna 3/10
Scott McKenzie 10/1
Ron McKernan 3/8, 9/8
Ian McLagan 5/12
Don McLean 10/2
Marshall McLuhan 7/21
Ed McMahon 3/6
Clyde McPhatter 6/13
Donald McPherson 7/4
Steve McQueen 3/24, 11/7
Christine McVie 7/12
John McVie 11/26
Margaret Mead 12/16
Pete Meadow 8/5
George Meany 8/16
Meat Loaf 9/27, 10/29
Meco 11/29
Bill Medley 9/19
Burgess Meredith 11/16
Randy Meisner 3/6
Melanie 2/3
John Cougar Mellencamp 10/7
Herman Melville 8/1
Memphis Slim 9/3
Sergio Mendez 2/11
Freddie Mercury 9/5
Ethel Merman 1/16
David Merrick 11/27
Jim Messina 11/12, 12/5
Mets 10/16
Michelangelo 3/6
Lee Michaels 11/24
Bette Midler 12/1
Midnight Special 2/2
Fred Milano 8/22
Buddy Miles 12/31
Arthur Miller 10/17
Glenn Miller 12/15
Roger Miller 1/2
Steve Miller 10/5
A.A. Milne 1/18
Little Milton 9/7, 12/31
Liza Minelli 3/12
Sal Mineo 1/10, 2/12
Charles Mingus 1/5, 4/22
Ho Chi Minh 5/19
Memphis Minnie 6/24
U.S. Mint 4/2
Ian Mitchell 8/22
Joni Mitchell 2/17, 9/27, 11/7
John Mitchell 11/1
Mitch Mitchell 6/9
Robert Mitchum 8/6

Mobile Fidelity 1/1, 2/1, 6/1, 9/1, 10/1
Moby Grape 6/17
Mohammed 4/20
Moody Blues 2/20
Robert A. Moog 5/23
The Moon 7/20
Keith Moon 8/23, 9/7
Clayton Moore 9/1
Hugh Moore 11/25
Mary Tyler Moore 12/29
Roger Moore 10/4
Sam Moore 10/12
Michael Monarch 6/5
Walter Mondale 1/5
Eddie Money 3/21
Thelonious Monk 2/17, 10/10
The Monkees 9/10, 9/12
Bill Monroe 9/13
James Monroe 4/28
Marilyn Monroe 6/1, 8/5
R. Mordian 1/1
Robert Morley 5/26
Nigel Morris 6/20
Jim Morrison 3/1, 3/2, 7/3, 8/4, 9/20, 12/8
Van Morrison 8/31
Samuel Morse 1/6, 4/27
Jelly Roll Morton 1/10, 7/10
Grandma Moses 9/7
Zero Mostel 2/28
Mountain 7/2
Mickey Mouse 2/14
Alphonse Mouzon 11/21
Wolfgang Amadeus Mozart 1/27
Maria Muldaur 9/12
Dave Mullen 10/3
Scott Muni 10/6, 12/18
Billy Murcia 11/6
Anne Murray 6/20
Dee Murray 4/3
Edward R. Murrow 4/25
David Muse 7/27
MUSE Concerts 9/19
Music Television (MTV) 8/1, 12/22, 12/31
Edmund Muskie 3/28
Benito Mussolini 4/28

N

Ralph Nader 2/27, 7/1
Jim Nabors 6/12
Ron Nagle 2/21
Joe Namath 5/31
Napoleon 4/20, 8/15

Graham Nash 2/2, 12/21
Johnny Nash 8/19
Jeff Neighbor 3/19
Rick Nelson 5/1, 5/8, 12/31
Sandy Nelson 12/1
Tracey Nelson 12/27
Willie Nelson 4/30
Anthony Newley 9/24
Paul Newman 1/26, 7/5
Randy Newman 11/28
Newport Folk Festival 6/20
Olivia Newton-John 9/26
New York City 7/13
Mike Nichols 11/6
George Nichopolous 9/18
Stevie Nicks 1/29, 5/26
Florence Nightingale 5/12
Don Nix 9/27
Richard Nixon 1/9, 2/21, 3/16, 4/17,
    9/26, 11/7, 11/8
Peter Noone 11/5
Gary Numan 3/8, 8/25
Rudolf Nureyev 3/17, 6/16
Laura Nyro 10/18

O

Annie Oakley 8/12
Berry Oakley 11/11
Phil Oakley 10/2
John Oates 4/7
Phil Ochs 4/9, 12/19
Odetta 12/31
Mike Oldfield 5/15
Davey O'List 12/13
Oliver 1/22
Laurence Olivier 5/22
Nigel Olssen 2/5
Eugene O'Neill 10/16
Yoko Ono 2/18, 5/26, 8/20, 11/29, 12/14
Roy Orbison 4/23, 6/6, 6/7, 8/29, 12/9
Oregon 10/5
Eugene Ormandy 11/18
George Orwell 1/21, 6/25
Ozzy Osbourne 1/20, 12/3
Gilbert O'Sullivan 12/1
Lee Oskar 3/24
Lee Harvey Oswald 11/24
Johnny Otis 12/28
Shuggie Otis 11/30
Peter O'Toole 8/2
Our Gang 7/30
Buck Owens 8/12
Jesse Owens 9/22
Ozzie & Harriet 10/3

P

Jack Paar 5/1
Pacific Phonograph Company 11/23
Al Pacino 4/25
David Pack 7/15
Geraldine Page 11/22
Jimmy Page 1/9, 10/19
Patti Page 11/8
Arnold Palmer 9/10
Carl Palmer 3/20, 12/30
Poli Palmer 5/25
Robert Palmer 1/19
Panama Canal 8/15
Jim Pankow 8/20
Joseph Papp 6/22
Felix Pappalardi 7/2
Rick Parfitt 10/12
Fred Paris 3/26
Charlie Parker 3/12, 8/30, 11/25
Fess Parker 8/16
Graham Parker 1/15
Jr. Parker 3/3
Tom Parker 6/26, 8/15
Van Dyke Parks 1/3
Fito de la Parra 2/8
Gene Parsons 4/9, 9/4
Graham Parsons 9/19, 11/5
Neil Part 12/12
Dolly Parton 1/19
Jaco Pastorius 12/1
Ed Patton 8/2
Floyd Patterson 9/25
Billy Paul 12/1
Les Paul 6/9
Tom Paxton 10/31
Bill Payne 3/12
Dennis Payton 8/11
Gregory Peck 4/5
Ann Peebles 4/27
Dave Pegg 11/2
Pele 10/23
John Pemberton 5/8
Teddy Pendergrass 3/18
William Penn 10/14
J.C. Penney 9/16
George Peppard 10/1
Carl Perkins 2/22, 4/9, 12/3
Steve Perron 8/8
Joe Perry 9/10
Steve Perry 1/22
Sylvia Peterson 9/30
Tom Petty 10/20
Dave Peverett 4/10
Esther Phillips 12/23

Jim Reeves 7/31
Della Reese 7/6
Martha Reeves 7/18
Keith Reid 10/10
Terry Reid 11/13
Keith Reif 11/14
Larry Reinhardt 7/7
Willie Reish 8/26
Burt Reiter 11/26
Lou Reizner 8/11
Rembrandt 7/15
Frederic Remington 10/4
Jean Renoir 9/15
REO Speedwagon 2/2
James Reston 11/3
Paul Revere 1/1, 4/18
Burt Reynolds 2/11
Debbie Reynolds 4/1, 9/26
Nick Reynolds 7/27
Rickie Lee Reynolds 10/28
Herbert Rhodes 10/1
Nick Rhodes 6/8
Tim Rice 11/10
Buddy Rich 6/30
Charlie Rich 12/4
Cliff Richard 10/14
Keith Richard 2/27, 12/18
Little Richard 3/8, 3/28, 12/3, 12/29, 12/31
J.P. Richardson 2/3, 10/24
Johnathan Richman 5/16
Gary Richratch 10/18
Eddie Rickenbacker 10/8
Don Rickles 5/8
Nelson Riddle 6/1
Greg Ridley 10/23
Jeannie C. Riley 10/19
Arthur Rimbaud 12/10
Rin Tin Tin 1/12, 7/1
Minnie Ripperton 7/12
Johnny Rivers 5/30, 11/7
Mac Roach 1/18
Jason Robards 7/22
Marty Robbins 9/26, 12/9
Gary Roberts 6/16
Rick Roberts 8/31
Cliff Robertson 7/5, 9/9
Robbie Robertson 7/5
Brooks Robinson 5/18
Edward G. Robinson 1/9, 12/12
Jackie Robinson 1/31
Smokey Robinson 2/19, 6/23
Tom Robinson 6/1
Maggie Roche 10/26

Suzzy Roche 9/29
Terre Roche 4/10
John D. Rockefeller 7/8
Nelson Rockefeller 7/8
Jim Rodford 7/7
Nile Rodgers 9/19
Paul Rodgers 12/12
Richard Rodgers 6/28, 12/30
Ginger Rogers 7/16
Jimmy Rogers 9/8
Kenny Rogers 8/21
Paul Rogers 12/2
Roy Rogers 11/5
Will Rogers 11/4
Rolling Stone Magazine 11/9
The Rolling Stones 1/6, 1/15, 1/18, 1/28, 2/11, 2/13, 3/14, 3/18, 4/16, 4/22, 4/29, 5/1, 5/10, 5/12, 5/27, 6/1, 6/3, 6/4, 6/7, 6/8, 6/14, 7/7, 7/30, 8/11, 8/24, 8/28, 9/29, 10/25, 11/1, 12/5, 12/6, 12/12, 12/18, 12/19
Rolling Thunder Revue 10/30
Max Romeo 2/8
Linda Ronstadt 6/12, 7/15, 8/21
Mickey Rooney 4/20, 9/23, 11/26
Eleanor Roosevelt 10/11
Franklin D. Roosevelt 1/30
Teddy Roosevelt 10/27
Tim Rose 9/23
Michael Rosen 10/8
Betsy Ross 1/1
Diana Ross 3/26
Mike Rossi 5/29
Gary Rossington 12/24
David Lee Roth 10/10
Johnny Rotten 1/31, 12/8
Richard Rountree 9/7
Lillian Roxon 8/9
Jerry Rubin 7/14
Arthur Rubinstein 1/28, 12/10
Jack Ruby 1/3
David Ruffin 1/18
Jimmy Ruffin 5/7
Todd Rundgren 6/22
Damon Runyon 10/4
Tom Rush 2/8
Willie Rush 8/26
Patrice Rushen 9/30
Joe Russell 9/25
Leon Russell 4/2
Lillian Russell 12/24
Russia 1/4
Babe Ruth 2/6
Mike Rutherford 10/2

Sonny & Cher 9/1
John Phillip Sousa 11/6
Joe South 2/28
Southside Johnny 12/4
The Specials 10/19
Phil Spector 2/10, 12/26
Ronnie Spector 8/10
Chris Spedding 6/17
Jeremy Spencer 7/4
Benjamin Spock 5/2
Dusty Springfield 4/16
Bruce Springsteen 5/29, 6/9, 6/10, 6/12,
    8/12, 9/23, 10/3, 10/27, 12/12, 12/22,
    12/31
Sputnik 10/4
Chris Squire 3/4
Robert Stack 1/13
Joseph Stalin 3/5, 12/21
Standells 4/23
Paul Stanley 1/20
Maurice Stans 3/21
Barbara Stanwyck 5/3, 7/16
Peter Staples 5/3
Pops Stables 12/28
Jason Starkey 8/19
Zak Starkey 9/13
Edwin Starr 1/21
Ringo Starr 2/11, 2/20, 4/27, 7/7, 8/16
Jefferson Starship 1/16, 5/12
John Steel 2/4
Tommy Steele 12/3, 12/17
Steely Dan 6/21
Rod Steiger 4/13
Gertrude Stein 2/3
Chris Stein 1/5
Mark Stein 3/11
John Steinbeck 2/27
Gloria Steinem 3/25
Casey Stengel 7/30
Isaac Stern 7/21
Cat Stevens 7/21, 9/9
Ray Stevens 1/24
Robert Louis Stevenson 11/13
Sly Stone 2/10, 3/15
Billy Stewart 1/17
James Stewart 7/9
Rod Stewart 1/10
Stephen Stills 1/3, 4/3, 7/9, 12/21, 12/23
Sting 10/2
Wally Stocker 3/27
Mike Stoller 3/13
Paul Stookey 11/30
Sam Strain 12/9
Johann Strauss 10/25

Igor Stravinsky 6/17
Barbra Streisand 3/26, 4/24
Keith Strickland 10/26
Joe Strummer 8/21
Chad Stuart 12/10
Styx 3/19
Suggs 1/13
Ed Sullivan 2/9, 5/12, 6/6, 9/25, 9/28,
    10/25
Donna Summer 12/31
Andy Summers 12/31
Superman 6/1
Sun Records 3/1, 12/3
Surfaris 6/22
Jacqueline Susann 8/20
David Susskind 12/19
Lord Sutch 11/10
Stu Sutcliffe 4/10
Joan Sutherland 11/7
Billy Swan 5/12
Gloria Swanson 3/27
Dave Swarbrick 4/5
Rachel Sweet 7/28
Jonathan Swift 11/30
Terry Sylvester 1/8
Tony Sylvester 10/7

T
Talking Heads 2/18
Garr Tallent 10/27
Nadra Talley 1/27
Richard Tandy 3/26
Sharon Tate /6, 8/9
Bernie Taupin 5/22
Andy T aylor 2/16
Derek Taylor 5/7
Elizabeth Taylor 2/27
James Taylor 3/12, 11/3
John Taylor 6/20
Larry Taylor 6/6
Livingston Taylor 11/21
Mick Taylor 1/27, 12/12
Roger Taylor 7/20
Vinnie Taylor 4/17
Zachary Taylor 11/24
Peter Illich Tchaikovsky 5/7
Richard Tee 11/24
Telephone 1/7
Television 1/27
Telstar 7/10, 7/23, 12/22
Ted Templeman 10/24
Toni Tennille 5/8
Studs Terkel 5/16
Joe Terranova 1/30

Eddie Vinson 12/18
Bobby Vinton 4/16
Miroslav Vitous 12/12
Voidoids 11/18
Jon Voight 12/29
Bob Vogle 1/16
Mark Volman 4/19
Harry Vonda 3/22
Kurt Vonnegut 11/11
Baron Von Richthofen 5/2
Dave Von Ronk 6/30

W

Wailers 11/4
Bunny Wailer 4/10
Loudon Wainwright III 9/5
John Waite 7/4
Tom Waits 12/7
Rick Wakeman 5/18
Eli Wallach 12/7
Narada Walden 4/23
Herschel Walker 2/23
Jerry Jeff Walker 3/16
T-Bone Walker 5/28
George Wallace 8/25
Mike Wallace 5/9
Fats Waller 12/15
Gordon Waller 6/4
Joe Walsh 11/20
Little Walter 2/15, 5/1
Barbara Walters 9/25
War of the Worlds 10/31
Bill Ward 5/5
Burt Ward 1/13
Andy Warhol 8/6
Clint Warwick 6/25
Alan Warner 4/21
Warren Commission 9/24
Dionne Warwick 12/12
Dinah Washington 8/29, 12/14
George Washington 2/22, 4/30, 9/16
Martha Washington 6/21
Ethel·Waters 10/31
Muddy Waters 4/14, 10/11
Roger Waters 9/6
Watkins Glen 7/28
Johnny Watson 2/3
Charlie Watts 6/2
Pete Watts 5/13
Fee Waybill 9/17
Carl Wayne 8/18
John Wayne 5/26, 6/11, 7/3
WEA Records 1/13
Captain Webb 8/24

Jack Webb 12/23
Jimmy Webb 12/5
Bob Welch 7/31
Raquel Welch 9/5
Kurt Weill 3/2, 4/4
Bob Weir 10/16
Orson Welles 5/6
H.G. Wells 9/21
Jr. Wells 12/9
Mary Wells 5/13
Max Weinberg 4/13
Adam West 7/2, 10/22
West Point 3/16
John Wetton 3/20
Jerry Wexler 1/10
Tina Weymouth 11/22
Wham-O 11/1
Where The Action Is 7/5
The Who 1/15, 3/25, 3/27, 5/10, 6/12,
    8/19, 9/22, 10/22, 12/4, 12/17
Whiskey-A-Go-Go 1/11
Bukka White 11/12
Chris White 3/7
Clarence White 6/7, 7/19
Ed White 6/3
Josh White 2/11
Lenny White 12/19
Maurice White 12/17, 12/19
Tony Joe White 7/23
Brad Whitford 2/23
Walt Whitman 5/32
Danny Whitten 11/18
Isle of Wight 8/26
Kim Wilde 11/18
Oscar Wilde 10/16
Thornton Wilder 4/17
Andy WIlliams 12/1
Ester Williams 8/8
Hank Williams 1/1, 9/17
Hank Williams, Jr. 3/7
John Williams 2/8
Maurice Williams 4/26
Paul Williams 8/17
Ted Williams 8/31
Tennessee Williams 3/26
Tommy Williams 4/5
Wendy O. Williams 1/18
Robin Williamson 11/24
Sonny Boy Williamson 11/6
Al Wilson 6/19, 9/3
Ann Wilson 6/19
Brian Wilson 6/20
Carl Wilson 12/21
Cindy Wilson 2/8

About The Authors

Sean Brickell has been a rock critic and columnist for *The Virginian-Pilot* in Norfolk, Virginia, and promotions manager for Atlantic Records and Elektra/Asylum Records. He has also helped manage national recording artists. He founded Brickell & Associates Public Relations in 1982, which has become the largest agency of its type in Virginia. At 39, he lives in Virginia Beach, Virginia with his wife Bean, children Alex and Lesley, au pair Samantha and his record and CD collection.

Rich Rothschild has been music director and an air personality for American University Radio, Washington, D.C. He worked for CBS Records in various marketing and merchandising capacities for over eight years. He currently owns RLR Associates, an advertising specialty company. A New Jersey native living in Maryland, at 34, he lives with his wife Lynda, daughter Lindsay and his record and compact disc collection.